Cottage Gardens

CASSELL'S GARDEN DIRECTORIES

Cottage Gardens

EVERYTHING YOU NEED TO CREATE A GARDEN

DAVID SQUIRE

Consultant Editor
LUCY HUNTINGTON

CASSELL&CO

First published in the United Kingdom in 2002 by CASSELL & CO

Design and text copyright © The Ivy Press Limited 2000

The moral right of David Squire to be identified as the author of this work has been
asserted in accordance with the Copyright, Designs and Patents Act of 1988.

A CIP Catalogue record for this book
is available from the British Library

ISBN 0 304 36233 6

This book was conceived,
designed and produced by
THE IVY PRESS LIMITED
The Old Candlemakers, West Street,
Lewes, East Sussex BN7 2NZ

Creative Director: PETER BRIDGEWATER
Designers: AXIS DESIGN
Editorial Director: SOPHIE COLLINS
Project Editor: ALISON COPLAND
Editor: CLAIRE MUSTERS
Illustrations: VANESSA LUFF & PETER BULL
Picture Researcher: LIZ EDDISON

Originated and printed in China by
Hong Kong Graphics and Printing Ltd

This book is typeset in 10.5/13 Linotype Perpetua and Univers

CASSELL & CO
Wellington House, 125 Strand, London WC2R 0BB

CONTENTS

INTRODUCTION

*E*ven *the term 'cottage garden' sounds idyllic, immediately conjuring up pictures of an informal garden, packed with floriferous annuals and herbaceous perennials, fruits and vegetables, and perhaps blossom from a flowering tree swaying in a gentle breeze. Ornamental wells, sundials, armillary spheres and beehives were added in the past as features that gave further interest to such gardens, while a white picket fence or a fragrant lavender hedge might have kept the whole scene united.*

The cottage-garden style still holds great appeal today and an increasing number of gardeners are incorporating the look into their own designs. One of its most pleasing qualities is that it creates a relaxing ambience, which helps to ease the strain of modern living. Informality is a main ingredient in the way cottage gardens are planted and this is

THEN AND NOW

🌢 Cottage-garden plants have a history of domestic use, and their fragrance was used worldwide to scent linen. In Europe, herbs such as lavender have long been used to give linen a fresh fragrance. In Japan and China, bundles of twigs of the deciduous and winter-flowering shrub wintersweet (*Chimonanthus praecox*) were used for the same purpose. Additionally, it was a custom for Chinese ladies to use the scented flowers to decorate their hair.

usually a less expensive way of gardening than buying large numbers of plants each year and adhering to a rigid pattern of planting. This is probably another important attraction for modern gardeners.

HISTORICAL ASSOCIATIONS

Cottage gardens are steeped in history and many of the plants have interesting stories. For example, the common gorse (*Ulex europaeus*) has long been a country shrub, and gorse wood and gorse charcoal were found in Neolithic sites, indicating that gorse was part of the great forests before they were cleared. In the last few centuries, gorse faggots were frequently used as fuel for heating bakers' ovens. It was also said that horses that fed on gorse developed whiskers on their lips. Gorse is a spectacular shrub and is very attractive when planted next to a post-and-rail type fence. It also has a romantic association; it flowers more or less throughout the year, giving rise to the old saying 'when gorse is out of bloom, kissing's out of season'.

LEFT *Trellis, chains and hanging baskets add extra height to this archetypal cottage-garden profusion of colourfully mingled flowers and plants of varying shapes and sizes.*

ABOVE *An ornamental fruit tree forms the centrepiece for this cleverly designed pattern of beds and borders packed with flowering plants from roses to Digitalis purpurea (foxgloves).*

CREATING A COTTAGE GARDEN

Gardening is a living and adaptable pastime and it is possible for everyone to discover the beauty of cottage-garden plants, both old and new, and to create a cottage garden all of their own. This book takes you through the processes of planning and designing your garden, selecting and buying suitable plants and carrying out the necessary practical tasks, as well as providing a comprehensive guide to a wide range of cottage-garden plants that should give you many years of pleasure.

HOW TO USE THIS BOOK

*C*assell's Garden Directories have been conceived and written to appeal both to gardening beginners and to confident gardeners who need advice for a specific project. Each book focuses on a particular type of garden, drawing on the experience of an established expert. The emphasis is on a practical and down-to-earth approach that takes account of the space, time and money that you have available. The ideas and techniques in these books will help you to produce an attractive and manageable garden that you will enjoy for years to come.

Cottage Gardens begins by exploring the history and traditions of cottage gardens. The rest of the book is divided into three sections. The opening section, Planning Your Garden, introduces the different types of cottage garden and looks at the effects that can be achieved and at some of the suitable plants available. There are also four specific inspirational garden plans for producing cottage gardens for different seasons and spaces.

Part Two, Creating a Cottage Garden, opens with a set of inspirational choices for different garden features, including paths and paving, arbours, arches and trellises, fences and walls and other traditional cottage-garden elements such as beehives, sundials and wells. From these, you can decide what features might be appropriate for your own cottage garden. The section then moves on to the practicalities of buying, propagating, maintaining and pruning cottage garden plants, with step-by-step explanations of the various basic techniques required and many useful hints

and tips. Moving on from this basic grounding, Part Two continues by giving advice on the different groups of plants, ranging from flowering plants such as annuals, biennials and herbaceous perennials to trees, shrubs, grass, herbs, fruit and vegetables. This section also encourages you to put your skills to work with a series of specific projects, such as creating a thyme path, making an ornamental well, planting a strawberry barrel and training a rose through a tree. Lists of 'star plants' are provided and techniques explained in simple terms.

The final part of the book, The Plant Directory, is a comprehensive listing of all the plants mentioned in the earlier sections, together with other plants that are ideal for use in a cottage garden. Each plant is illustrated in colour, and there is information on appropriate growing conditions, speed of growth and ease of maintenance. A coloured bar tells you, at a glance, in which seasons a listed plant is at its most attractive.

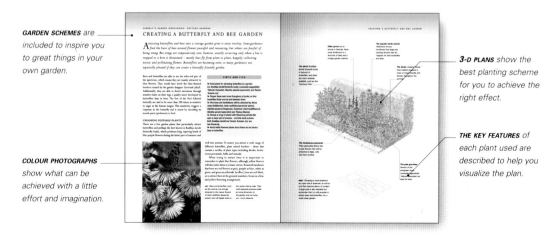

GARDEN SCHEMES are included to inspire you to great things in your own garden.

COLOUR PHOTOGRAPHS show what can be achieved with a little effort and imagination.

3-D PLANS show the best planting scheme for you to achieve the right effect.

THE KEY FEATURES of each plant used are described to help you visualize the plan.

CHOICES SPREADS show a selection of plants, garden furniture or other features that may be appropriate in your garden.

THE CHECKLIST details important things to look out for in choosing garden features, or suitable plants to complement them.

PRACTICAL SPREADS give useful information on basic techniques and garden projects.

CLEAR ILLUSTRATIONS show each step of the process.

COLOUR PHOTOGRAPHS help you to decide on appropriate features for your garden.

EXPLANATORY TEXT describes the various possibilities available in each category.

WATCHPOINTS BOXES give a checklist of cautions and problems to look out for.

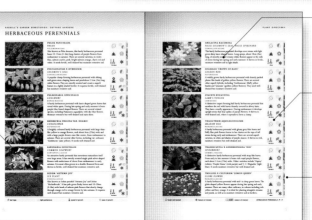

THE PLANT DIRECTORY is organized into categories making it simple to find a particular type of plant.

COLOUR PHOTOGRAPHS clearly identify each plant listed.

CLEAR DESCRIPTIVE TEXT details the appearance and the appropriate growing conditions for each plant.

THE SYMBOLS PANEL gives important information on features such as speed of growth and shade tolerance.

SIDEBAR shows at a glance the season of interest for each plant.

PLANNING YOUR GARDEN

1

Cottage gardens, with their relaxed and informal nature, never fail to capture attention and to create a nostalgia for past times when life seemed simpler. Like other garden styles, though, the nature of cottage gardens has developed and changed. Nowadays we can choose whether to recreate a completely traditional garden, or consider a modern version that is a fusion of the old and the new. Whichever you pick, romance and tradition are always important elements of the cottage style.

LEFT *An old stone font stands out proudly in the midst of a rich, dense planting of, amongst others, irises, alliums, lavender, geums and peonies.*

THE HISTORY OF THE COTTAGE GARDEN

*F*ew styles of gardening have such a relaxed and informal nature as the cottage garden. With a rich medley of flowers, fruits, vegetables and herbs it evokes an earlier age when, for country people, life was closely woven around the seasons. To many people, the cottage garden signifies social cohesion and well-being, and a continuity of gardening that reaches back over many centuries. But is this a true reflection?

During the early 1800s, the English romantic poet Robert Southey (1774–1843) wrote of a decaying society, at the same time eulogizing old stone cottages with gardens bursting with flowers, fruits and vegetables. However, Thomas Macaulay (1800–59), English historian, poet and statesman, saw things differently and questioned whether the cottage garden was a genuine feature of earlier English life, or rather solely a nineteenth-century invention.

Part of the confusion stemmed from gardening terminology; the English nobility often retreated to 'country cottages and villas' that were clearly more extensive and lavish than a farm worker's dwelling. Similar confusion was present in North America, where 'cottage' and 'villa' were frequently used synonymously. The Irishman Bernard

THEN AND NOW

❧ It is claimed that an Act passed during the Elizabethan period forbade cottages to be constructed unless a certain amount of land surrounded each one of them. The Act stated that all cottages failing in this respect were henceforth to be called 'silly cottages'.

McMahon (c.1775–1816) settled in Philadelphia and in 1806 published *The American Gardener's Calendar* in which he wrote of villa gardens. He suggested that in these gardens a few people preferred an arrangement of purely ornamental plants, but that the majority of gardeners '… wish to have a little of everything – vegetables, fruit, flowers and ornamental trees'.

In the mid-nineteenth century, the Scottish-born gardener and journalist Donald Beaton wrote that there was a wealth of superb cottage gardens and that 'they were all made and planted within the last twenty years'. There is, indeed, little to indicate that cottage gardens, as we know them today, existed before the end of the eighteenth century. It was not until the nineteenth century that front gardens, which are by far the most pictured aspects of cottage gardens, became possible. This, in part, resulted from the Parliamentary Enclosures Act that constrained animals to fields and allowed landowners to erect fences. Improvements to road surfaces also made it possible to define the boundaries of front gardens more clearly.

LEFT *Apples* (Malus domestica) *have been cultivated in cottage gardens since the beginning of the eighteenth century. Some* *of the early varieties, such as 'Annie Elizabeth', which was first grown in 1866, are still available today.*

FOOD OR FLOWERS?

The idealist's cottage garden was, and perhaps always will be, a medley of flowering plants – annuals, herbaceous perennials, floriferous shrubs and trees burgeoning with blossom. During the early and middle part of the nineteenth century, however, reformers advocated the growing of vegetables and fruit. In part this was a result of the efforts of the Young England movement, which campaigned in the 1830s and 1840s for the provision of allotments. Many new varieties of fruit were introduced in the nineteenth century and some of these are still available today.

Vegetables were frequently grown in rows in early cottage gardens, and those with attractive foliage created shape and colour contrasts to other plants. Broad beans, with their silver sheen, became an attractive feature when sown against a background of rhubarb leaves. Lettuces were grown with a backdrop of bulbing onions. In the mid-nineteenth century, flower seeds became increasingly available from the many seed companies that were being formed during that time. This encouraged gardeners also to grow annuals and perennials from seeds, creating the mix of food and flowers popular today.

ABOVE *The 'traditional' cottage garden mixes several elements – ornaments, flowers and produce. In this modern version, climbers and perennials mingling with strawberries and roses are offset by the eye-catching urn.*

THEN AND NOW

❧ Until the eighteenth century, honey was the principal source of sweetness. It was widely used in country cottages to cure hams and to preserve other foods. Bees were seen to be so valuable that it was essential to keep them happy and contented. This involved the custom of telling them of momentous family events such as births and deaths. It also became a tradition for white ribbons to be tied around hives on wedding days.

❧ These customs were carefully followed in England, as well as in early settled parts of North America. When selling bees it was also essential that a gold coin be offered, rather than bartering with corn or a small pig. This led to the saying:

If you wish your bees to thrive,
Gold must be paid for every hive;
For when they're bought with other money,
There will be neither swarm nor honey.

EARLY COTTAGE GARDEN PLANTS

Cottage gardens during the early eighteenth century were often filled with so-called 'traditional' plants. These encompassed native plants as well as those introduced into gardens by the Romans and later grown and protected in monasteries during the Dark Ages and up until the beginning of the Renaissance. Some plants, such as Alcea rosea (hollyhocks), are thought to have been first brought into Britain by the Crusaders during the early centuries of the last millennium.

For many centuries monastic gardens were repositories of plants – especially those with medicinal or culinary qualities. Monasteries exchanged plants and seeds with other religious establishments and also supplied many secular gardens. It was in the eighteenth century, however, that nurserymen started to play a role in propagating plants, as well as growing plants from foreign lands.

For many centuries plants had been introduced into Britain from mainland Europe. In the early seventeenth century, French nurserymen issued catalogues of plants for

sale, and a few years later the Dutch established a trade in bulbs. It was with the main introduction of North American plants in the eighteenth century, however, that trade in plants burgeoned.

COTTAGE GARDEN TOPIARY

Topiary is a craft that has been pursued for at least 2,000 years. It was well known to the Roman naturalist and writer Pliny the Elder (AD 23–79), who wrote of magnificent hunting scenes and ships expertly clipped out of cypress. The Romans introduced topiaries to northern Europe and Britain and featured them in their villa gardens. When they left, topiary was mainly practised in monasteries and, in later years, in Elizabethan gardens. During the eighteenth century, large stately homes continued the craft, mainly forming regular shapes such as spheres, cones and squares. It was left to cottage gardens to add a

LEFT *Cottage gardens need not always look completely informal. This bird bath is reached by means of a soft green path of Chamaemelum nobile (chamomile), edged by low clipped hedges and areas of gravel with sunken pots.*

more amusing side to the art, and it was here that the shapes of animals and birds were first formed. Creating a topiary figure is a long-term project and one that can take several years. Basic shapes are created from wire frameworks, with regular clipping and pinching out of shoots to produce a detailed figure.

PUBLICIZING COTTAGE-GARDEN PLANTS

Towards the middle of the nineteenth century there was an increasing demand for information about designing and planting cottage gardens. *The Cottage Gardener's Dictionary* was published in 1847 and the magazine *The Cottage Gardener* appeared in 1848. The Irish garden writer and designer William Robinson (1838–1935) wrote about cottage gardens, and in *The English Flower Garden* (1883) he claimed that it was only in cottage gardens that flowers could be grown in a natural way. Gertrude Jekyll (1843–1932) wrote a plethora of books extolling the informal use of flowering plants. She recognized the wide-ranging influence of cottage gardens and the debt all garden designers owed to them.

ABOVE *In this garden the juxtaposition of tall columnar conifers with low-growing clipped evergreens creates an unusual feature with an architectural look that contrasts well with the more relaxed areas of planting.*

POINTS TO CONSIDER

❧ Boundary hedges create barriers to animals as well as reducing the impact of the wind and lessening the risk of cold wind searing the foliage of tender plants. They are especially needed in exposed areas. Solid barriers, such as walls and fences, create strong eddies on their lee sides, whereas hedges filter the wind. A hedge's effectiveness can be felt at a distance of up to 30 times its height, although the major benefit is within the first third of this distance. A robust boundary hedge can be formed by *Crataegus monogyna* (common hawthorn, or may). *Fagus sylvatica* (common beech) is another good external hedge, with the bonus that the leaves assume rich shades in autumn.

❧ Internal hedges do not need to be as robust as external ones and are ideal for separating one part of a garden from another. They can be formed of foliage shrubs, as well as those better known for their flowers.

COTTAGE GARDEN PLANTS TODAY

*E*arly cottage gardens were reflections of an age when time for maintenance was accepted as essential and informality signified well-being. Today the situation has changed. There are many more cottage garden plants available and buying and planting them has been made easier. Nurseries specializing in cottage garden plants produce mail-order catalogues and local garden centres also offer a wide range.

The number of cottage garden plants available is now enormous, but still includes many old favourites. Indeed, cottage gardens rely on herbaceous plants that came from North America more than a century ago, including *Coreopsis verticillata* (introduced in 1759), *Echinacea purpurea* (purple cone flower, 1699) and *Erigeron speciosus* (fleabane, 1838).

Many bulbous plants have also found their way into cottage gardens. They often come from hot areas where the soil is poor and, for long periods, dry. Tulips were grown as garden flowers in Turkey at about the beginning of the sixteenth century. In the 1630s the Dutch developed a love affair with tulips and fortunes were made and lost speculating over them. These plants eventually arrived in Britain and were then introduced into cottage gardens, where they have thrived ever since. Trees form the frame-

work of cottage gardens and their range encompasses those from North America, Europe, Asia and China. Additionally, some of the flowering trees seen in today's cottage gardens are hybrids that have been developed in recent times. *Prunus* 'Accolade' originated in the 1930s, while *Prunus* 'Taihaku' (great white cherry), though extinct in its native Japan, was discovered in a Sussex garden in 1900.

NEW ROSES

Cottage gardens would not be complete without a few shrub roses filling borders with colour, or one or two climbers or ramblers swamping arbours and trellises with both colour and scent. Few early cottage gardens were without either *Rosa gallica* 'Versicolor', popularly known as *Rosa mundi*, or *Rosa rubiginosa*, the famous eglantine or

LEFT *A cottage garden feel can be created in the smallest spaces – here varied pots of summer bedding plants combine in a delightful mishmash of vibrant colours.*

ABOVE Rosa gallica *'Versicolor'* is a old cottage-garden stalwart, and if you sit beside it on a warm summer's evening it will reward you with a rich, intoxicating fragrance.

sweet briar. In recent years New English roses have been bred that combine the recurrent flowering qualities and wide colour range of Modern roses with the charm and form of Old roses. Many of these new roses have a superb and unusual fragrance. There are a number of excellent varieties and some of these are featured on pages 92–3.

Climbing and rambling roses have been developed over many years: the climber 'Aimée Vibert' originated in 1828, the rambler 'Alexander Girault' in 1909, and in 1961 the climbing New English rose 'Constance Spry' was created. This particular climber can also be grown as a shrub rose in a border.

POINTS TO CONSIDER

There are many different colour combinations to add a feast of colour to borders:

🍂 For a salmon, orange-red and yellow mixture try a carpet of salmon-coloured *Erysimum cheiri* (wallflowers) and a mixture of yellow cottage-type tulips.

🍂 For a blue, scarlet and gold mixture plant a selection of pale blue *Myosotis sylvatica* (forget-me-nots) and the scarlet and gold single early tulip 'Keizerskroon'.

🍂 For a combination of white and blue plant a dense carpet of the biennial *Bellis perennis* (common daisy) and blue parrot-type tulips.

🍂 For a medley of shades of blue, in autumn plant several varieties of *Myosotis sylvatica* (forget-me-not) to form irregular patterns. They create a dense covering.

FLOWERING FRONT GARDENS

*T*he traditional front garden, open to view and divided by a brick or paved path, has always been the conventional vision of a 'typical' cottage plot. Spreading trees, paths edged with lavender hedges and picket fences are all part of this idyllic scene. Creating a colourful display for spring and early summer is a good way to welcome the onset of better weather. In autumn, however, when winter looms, it is also important to have an attractive, carefully planted front garden to cheer yourself up.

Gardens always benefit from careful planning and nothing is as important as ensuring you have a variety of plants in flower for as much of the year as possible. It is often best to plant seasonal flowering groups. When you do this, you must consider the flowering times of the plants you choose for each group, so that they will create a beautiful display together. In the plan opposite, the spring-flowering plants have been carefully chosen for complementary flowering times so that they will produce a feast of colour. Below are a few suggestions for plantings throughout the year.

FLOWERS FOR A SPRINGTIME DISPLAY

The hardy, deciduous shrub *Forsythia* x *intermedia* (golden bells) flowers during early and mid-spring and creates a mass of golden-yellow bell-shaped flowers. Try planting small groups of red tulips around it. Space the individual bulbs about 15cm (6in) apart. The variety 'Fritz Kreisler' is

POINTS TO CONSIDER

It is worth adding structures such as arches to the front garden. These lead people through to the door, and provide a base for plants (such as those listed here) to grow on.
- *Hedera canariensis* 'Glorie de Marengo'.
- *Hedera colchica* 'Sulphur Heart' for trellises or large arches.
- *Humulus lupulus* 'Aureus' – ideal for growing on a wind-buffeted arch.

superb. Ornamental crab apples, such as *Malus* x *purpurea* 'Eleyi', which grow well in full sun, are enhanced by a frill of *Erysimum cheiri* (wallflowers) positioned towards the outer edges of their branches.

SUMMER FLOWERS

The hardy, basal-rooting *Lilium candidum* (madonna lily) flowers during early and midsummer, with slender stems topped by pure white, bell-shaped flowers. It is an ideal companion for *Digitalis purpurea* (foxgloves), which have tall stems of flowers in a colour range from purple, through pink to red. The two plants form an attractive colour and shape contrast.

CREATING AN AUTUMN DISPLAY

A bold and unusual duo for early and mid-autumn is the evergreen *Sedum* 'Autumn Joy' and the bulbous *Colchicum* 'Waterlily'. The heads of the sedum change from salmon-pink through orange-red to orange-brown, while the colchicum has mauve flowers.

LEFT *There are many summer-flowering plants suitable for a cottage garden. Trial and error will help you choose the best – enjoy experimenting to find your favourites.*

Give height to the garden
with an ornamental tree like
Malus x purpurea 'Eleyi'
(crab apple), which provides
purple spring flowers and
autumn fruits.

When the daffodils under
the window have faded,
Nigella damascena (love-in-a-
mist) on the other side of the
path will take over.

For year-round interest,
grow a variegated ivy such
as Hedera colchica 'Sulphur
Heart' around the front door.

In spring, daffodils
and tulips will give a
bright and long-lasting
display, and work well
in combination with
Convallaria majalis (lily-
of-the-valley).

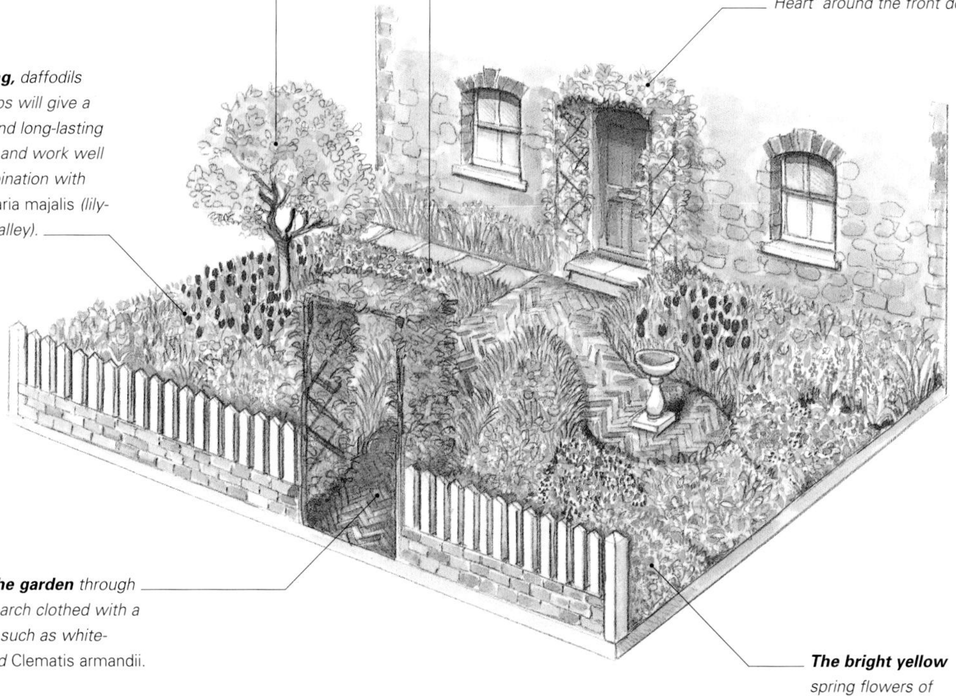

Enter the garden through
a rustic arch clothed with a
climber such as white-
flowered Clematis armandii.

The bright yellow
spring flowers of
Forsythia x intermedia
complement the use
of daffodils throughout
the planting scheme.

RIGHT An ornamental water feature is
central to the timeless nature of this plan,
while the picket fencing adds a boundary
frill to mark the garden's perimeter.

CREATING A BUTTERFLY AND BEE GARDEN

Attracting butterflies and bees into a cottage garden gives it extra vitality. Some gardeners find the buzz of bees around flowers peaceful and reassuring, but others are fearful of being stung. Bee stings are comparatively rare, however, usually occurring only when a bee is trapped or a hive is threatened – mostly bees fly from plant to plant, happily collecting nectar and pollinating flowers. Butterflies are becoming rarer, so many gardeners are especially pleased if they can create a butterfly-friendly garden.

Bees and butterflies are able to see the infra-red part of the spectrum, which means they are mainly attracted to blue flowers. They would have loved the blue-themed borders created by the garden designer Gertrude Jekyll. Additionally, they are able to detect sweetness through sensitive hairs on their legs, a quality more developed in butterflies than in bees. The feet of the Red Admiral butterfly are said to be more than 200 times as sensitive to sugar as the human tongue. This sensitivity triggers a response in the butterfly and it reacts by uncoiling its mouth parts (proboscis) to feed.

CHOOSING SUITABLE PLANTS

There are a few garden plants that particularly attract butterflies and perhaps the best known is *Buddleja davidii* (butterfly bush), which produces long, tapering heads of lilac-purple flowers during the latter part of summer and

well into autumn. To ensure you attract a wide range of different butterflies, plant mixed borders – those that contain a medley of plant types including shrubs, herbaceous perennials, bulbs and annuals.

When trying to attract bees it is important to remember to plant blue flowers, although yellow flowers will also entice them to a lesser extent. Research has shown that bees see red flowers as grey, purple as blue, white as green, and green as yellowish. In effect, bees are red-blind, so to attract them in the greatest numbers, focus on a blue and yellow flowering arrangement.

LEFT *Bees and butterflies are strongly attracted to the mauve flowers of* Aster sedifolius *(perennial asters).* *Their vivid seasonal presence adds an extra dimension to the garden and can bring you much pleasure.*

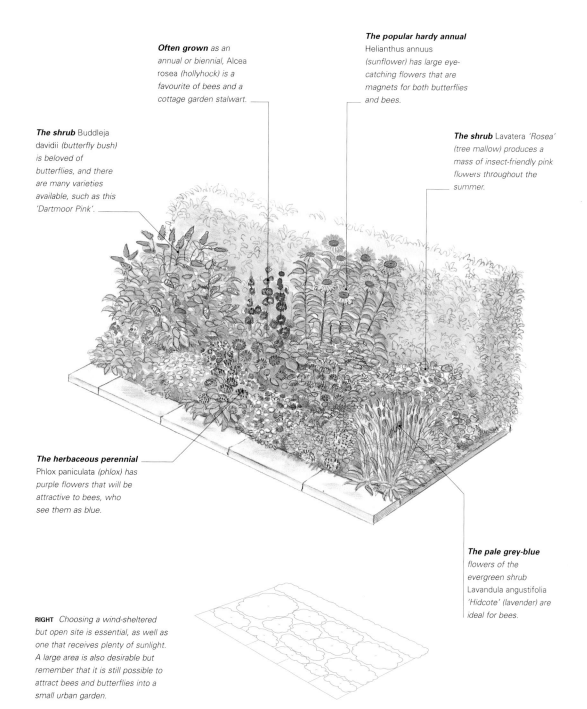

Often grown as an annual or biennial, Alcea rosea (hollyhock) is a favourite of bees and a cottage garden stalwart.

The popular hardy annual Helianthus annuus (sunflower) has large eye-catching flowers that are magnets for both butterflies and bees.

The shrub Buddleja davidii (butterfly bush) is beloved of butterflies, and there are many varieties available, such as this 'Dartmoor Pink'.

The shrub Lavatera 'Rosea' (tree mallow) produces a mass of insect-friendly pink flowers throughout the summer.

The herbaceous perennial Phlox paniculata (phlox) has purple flowers that will be attractive to bees, who see them as blue.

The pale grey-blue flowers of the evergreen shrub Lavandula angustifolia 'Hidcote' (lavender) are ideal for bees.

RIGHT Choosing a wind-sheltered but open site is essential, as well as one that receives plenty of sunlight. A large area is also desirable but remember that it is still possible to attract bees and butterflies into a small urban garden.

THE ROMANTIC COTTAGE GARDEN

*R*omance in a key theme in the cottage garden. Cloistered arbours provide secluded places, while plants with romantic associations add mystery. Several climbers that are perfect for arbours have this quality, and perhaps none more so than Clematis flammula, the fragrant virgin's bower. Some climbers, such as 'woodbine' or honeysuckle (Lonicera periclymenum), have been romanticized by Shakespeare. Other plants have acquired romantic common names, such as love-in-a-mist (Nigella damascena).

When siting an arbour, choose a sheltered position in either full sun or only partial shade. A westerly orientation will allow you to enjoy the last rays of light during still summer evenings, while a background formed by an evergreen hedge or a wall gives protection against blustery winds. It also helps to prevent the rapid dispersal of fragrance from scented plants you plan to grow over the arbour.

A wide range of arbours is available. Some have integral seats, while others provide space for the inclusion of a rustic bench. It is also important to think about how to reach the arbour if it is at the bottom of the garden. A firm, all-weather path is desirable. You should also consider the view both to and from the arbour.

ROMANTIC ROSE COMBINATIONS

Roses are perfect for an arbour, and can be planted in many attractive combinations. For example, for a large arbour, plant a combination of *Clematis chrysocoma* and the climbing rose 'Helen Knight'. The clematis is ideal for clothing a wall behind an arbour, as well as sprawling over it. In summer it bears white flowers tinged with pink. 'Helen Knight' will also clamber over the arbour, where it will bear clear yellow flowers in early summer.

The Damask rose 'Madame Hardy' bears white flowers with a lemon-like fragrance in midsummer. It makes a superb background for the several pink varieties of the herbaceous perennial *Geranium endressii*. The Bourbon rose 'Madame Isaac Pereire' has a bushy habit, and richly fragrant, madder-crimson flowers. It is an ideal companion for lilies, double peonies and *Syringa* (lilac).

LEFT *A sheltered arbour, clothed in red roses, makes the perfect place for a secret tryst – this arbour comes complete with a lookout in the form of a fine sculpted dog.*

The fragrant climbing rose 'Zéphirine Drouhin' bears rose-pink flowers that contrast with the rose on the other side of the arbour.

The arbour is clothed with the white-flowered Clematis flammula and Clematis chrysocoma – the latter's flowers are tinged with pink.

It is hard to imagine a more delicate – or romantically named – plant than Nigella damascena (love-in-a-mist).

The blooms of this climbing rose, 'Helen Knight', are of a bright, clear yellow, and complement the two clematis on the arbour.

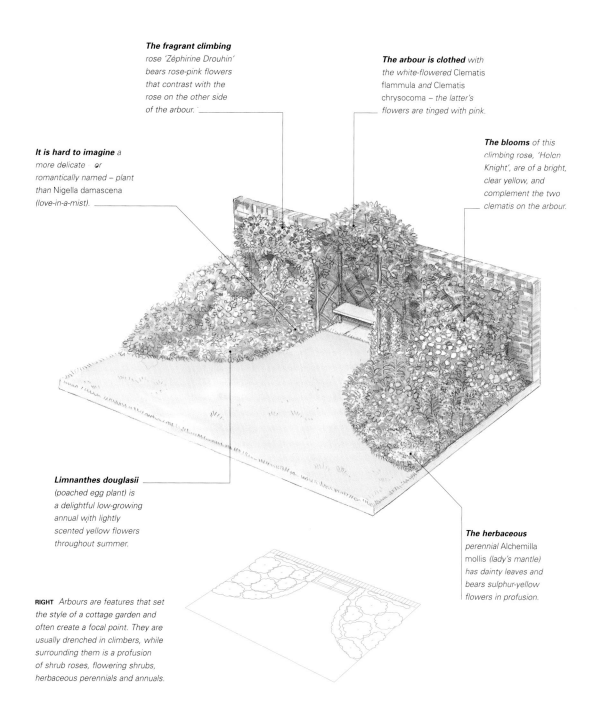

Limnanthes douglasii (poached egg plant) is a delightful low-growing annual with lightly scented yellow flowers throughout summer.

The herbaceous perennial Alchemilla mollis (lady's mantle) has dainty leaves and bears sulphur-yellow flowers in profusion.

RIGHT Arbours are features that set the style of a cottage garden and often create a focal point. They are usually drenched in climbers, while surrounding them is a profusion of shrub roses, flowering shrubs, herbaceous perennials and annuals.

A GLORIOUS SUMMER FLOWER GARDEN

Flower-packed summer borders that display a riot of colour epitomize the popular conception of cottage gardens. Old gnarled apple trees, perhaps past their best, may form supports over which roses and other climbers can be trained. Even if there are no trees, a tripod of roughly cut wood, or a tall, thick rustic pole, will provide support for a rose such as 'Zéphirine Drouhin', which produces fragrant deep rose-pink flowers throughout most of summer and even into early autumn. The borders themselves can be packed with shrubs, perennials, annuals and bulbs to produce a spectacular show.

When planning your summer-flowering cottage garden, take into consideration its size. If it is large, plant dominant clusters of herbaceous plants, with three or more of the same type of plant grouped together. In a small garden it may be more realistic to use just one plant of a dominant subject, along with two or three smaller plants. Low-growing plants at the edges of a border should always be placed in groups of at least three, because they are viewed from above while those at the middle and back are seen from their sides. If the latter are tall, they fill sufficient vertical space to offset their single-planted nature.

Evergreen shrubs with variegated leaves will brighten a border throughout the year; gold and yellow variegated shrubs are especially attractive when grown in full sun,

but do not let them dominate the other plants. Cottage gardens look their best when packed with colour, but try to avoid too many shades that fight for attention. Some deciduous shrubs, such as weigela, have forms with coloured or variegated leaves which are less dramatic than their evergreen counterparts. They are therefore more easily placed in a border, and their flowers are a bonus.

BACKGROUND INFLUENCES

Where flower borders have a wall or a house behind them, take this into consideration when planning which colours to plant there. A white cottage wall creates a bright backdrop, even in winter. Yellow, gold, scarlet or green flowers are at their most dramatic against this background. Green is an unusual flower colour, but one plant that provides it is *Amaranthus caudatus* 'Viridis'.

Grey stone walls are less dominant, and deep-blue or purple, pink or red flowers work ideally against them. Red brick walls will show off white, soft-blue, silver or lemon flowers to perfection.

LEFT *Planting in groups will produce a lively, casual effect in which blocks of colour combine and contrast with their neighbours in a seemingly random way.*

This old apple tree has been rejuvenated and enlivened by the addition of the climbing rose 'Zéphirine Drouhin'.

Taller-growing plants such as this lemon-scented Damask rose 'Madame Hardy' should be placed in the centre of the bed.

The herbaceous perennial Hosta fortunei *var.* albopicta (plantain lily) is mainly grown for its strikingly variegated leaves.

Helichrysum italicum (curry plant) is a low-growing shrub with aromatic, silvery-grey foliage.

Sedum 'Autumn Joy' (ice plant) is a late-flowering, low-growing perennial that is ideal for the edge of the border.

Nepeta x faasennii (catmint) has long spires of lavender-blue flowers throughout the summer.

RIGHT This bed has been designed to look good from any angle, but the best view of all is from the windows of the house.

CREATING A COTTAGE GARDEN

2

The charming informality of cottage gardens is relatively simple to create if you have planned carefully before you start. This section provides clear and practical information, first about basic features such as paths, patios, arbours and arches, tunnels, trellises, fences and walls. It then explains how to choose the right plants for your site and how to plant and care for them. Interesting and unusual practical projects are included, from planting a thyme path to creating an ornamental well.

LEFT *Glorious displays of summer colour are the result of careful planning and good plant care.*

FLOORING • CHOICES

❶

STONE PAVING

Stone paving creates an all-weather surface for patios and paths. For many years, natural stone paving was popular; it still suits cottage gardens and other informal areas, but is expensive and often difficult to obtain.

Slabs formed of reconstituted stone or concrete are a good alternative. They are available in several sizes and shapes and can be used to create informal patterns. For cottage gardens, avoid those with smooth or highly coloured surfaces.

Where spaces are left between paving slabs, it is a nice idea to plant low-growing plants such as thyme in the gaps. Position them towards the outer edges of the path so that the chance of them being stepped on is less.

CHOICE PLANTS CHECKLIST	
❧ *Erica carnea* (winter-flowering heather): use the low-growing varieties	❧ *Thymus serpyllum* (wild thyme)
❧ *Limnanthes douglasii* (poached egg plant) can be sown between slabs	❧ *Thymus vulgaris* (common thyme)

❷

BRICKS

Bricks have been used for centuries to form cottage garden paths. They can be laid either on an edge or with the 'face' side uppermost, in straight lines or in a variety of patterns. Some, such as the interlinking herringbone pattern, increase the path's stability as well as adding visual interest.

New or second-hand bricks can be used, but ordinary house bricks are too porous and disintegrate after a few years of frost and rain. Instead, use 'specials' (used in engineering, they are a much harder-wearing type of brick which will not crumble with hard weather or wear).

For decoration, rather than placing plants between individual bricks, you could plant a low, flowering hedge of lavender along each side.

CHOICE PLANTS CHECKLIST	
❧ *Dianthus barbatus* (sweet william)	❧ *Lavandula angustifolia* 'Hidcote' (lavender)
❧ *Heliotropium arborescens* (cherry pie)	❧ *Limnanthes douglasii* (poached egg plant)
❧ *Ipheion uniflorum* (spring starflower)	

❸

GRAVEL AND SHINGLE PATHS

These are more informal than brick, and readily harmonize with cottage gardens. They are easily constructed, but must have strong constraints along the sides to prevent the gravel or shingle spreading. For an informal appearance, use an edging of logs about 7.5–13cm (3–4in) thick. Flat areas suit these materials best, as on slopes they tend to slip downhill. Young children may find the gravel fascinating, and tend to scatter it. Nevertheless, it has an attractive appearance, which changes in varying light, especially after rain.

The edges can be softened by planting shrubs with a cascading and spreading habit along the edges. When planting, allow for each plant to double its spread.

CHOICE PLANTS CHECKLIST	
❧ *Ceratostigma willmottianum* (hardy plumbago)	❧ *Forsythia* x *intermedia* (golden bells)
❧ *Cistus* x *dansereaui* (rock rose)	❧ *Genista hispanica* (Spanish gorse)
	❧ *Helichrysum italicum* (curry plant)

❹

CRAZY-PAVING PATHS

Crazy paving is not an 'ancient' material and if employed excessively in a cottage garden becomes overpowering. However, when used to form paths 90cm–1.2m (3–4ft) wide, and draped at the sides with spreading and cascading plants, it is suitable. When a crazy-paving path is constructed in a lawn the grass forms an attractive edging.

Unlike other path materials, it is ideal for use on undulating areas and where an irregularly shaped path is needed. To make it attractive, try using a few coloured pieces of crazy paving set among those with a normal concrete colour. Because the path forms a 'solid' surface — unlike gravel and shingle where water drains freely — ensure there is a slight slope towards the edges.

CHOICE PLANTS CHECKLIST	
❧ *Ceratostigma willmottianum* (hardy plumbago)	❧ *Hydrangea macrophylla* (common hydrangea)
❧ *Fuchsia magellanica* (lady's eardrops)	❧ *Limnanthes douglasii* (poached egg plant)
	❧ *Potentilla fruticosa* (shrubby cinquefoil)

VERTICAL ELEMENTS • CHOICES

❶

ARBOURS AND ROMANTIC BOWERS

Arbours and romantic bowers make delightful additions to cottage gardens, especially when clothed in scented flowers such as *Clematis flammula* (fragrant virgin's bower). Using leafy climbers will help to create a cloistered feature.

There are several types of arbour to consider; some can be integrated into trellises or placed against walls or hedges. Others are best used as corner units on a patio or in another secluded place. Free-standing types can be positioned in the centre of a garden.

Wherever you decide to place your arbour, it is important to consider the whole space. Think about the view that will be seen *from* the arbour as well as around it, and then select suitable plants.

CHOICE PLANTS CHECKLIST

❧ *Clematis flammula* (fragrant virgin's bower)
❧ *Humulus lupulus* 'Aureus' (yellow-leaved hop)
❧ *Jasminum officinale* (common white jasmine)

❧ *Lonicera periclymenum* 'Belgica' (early Dutch honeysuckle) and 'Serotina' (late Dutch honeysuckle).
❧ *Vitis vinifera* 'Purpurea' (purple-leaved grapevine)

❷

ARCHES

Arches can be used to create an air of mystery in the garden by screening off separate areas yet at the same time providing a glimpse of what lies beyond. They are also ideal for displaying colourful plants at head height.

Stone or brick walls with arches built into them are more permanent than free-standing arches formed of wood or metal, but even the latter will last for upwards of 20 years. Metal arches may be ornate and delicate whereas rustic wooden types have a 'chunky' and relaxed nature that especially suits large cottage gardens. Planed wooden arches are also suitable, but need to be drenched in flowering or foliage climbers to ensure that they harmonize with other features.

CHOICE PLANTS CHECKLIST

❧ *Clematis flammula* (fragrant virgin's bower)
❧ *Humulus lupulus* 'Aureus' (yellow-leaved hop)

❧ *Jasminum officinale* (common white jasmine)
❧ *Lonicera periclymenum* 'Belgica' (early Dutch honeysuckle)

❸

TUNNELS

Tunnels are unusual features in cottage gardens and can look dramatic when densely covered with roses or pendulous clusters of laburnum flowers. They are ideal for channelling people from one part of a garden to another, and if a sundial, ornamental well or seat is positioned at the far end of the tunnel it will create an attractive focal point.

Ready-made tunnels are available in widths ranging from 1.5m (5ft) to 4.8m (16ft), and in shapes including round, gothic and Roman. Lengths are variable but it is best to avoid exceptionally long ones.

Apple and pear walks, formed of metal arches straddling a path, were popular in kitchen gardens during Victorian times.

CHOICE PLANTS CHECKLIST	
❧ Apple and pear trees – a range of varieties are suitable	❧ *Rosa* 'Madame Grégoire Staechelin'
❧ *Laburnum* x *watereri* 'Vossii' (golden rain tree)	❧ *Rosa* 'Zéphirine Drouhin'
	❧ *Wisteria* – the white and violet-blue forms

❹

TRELLISES

Trellises vary in style. Some are formal, made of planed wood and either secured to a wall or attached to posts to form a free-standing screen. Others are constructed from rustic poles, usually placed alongside a path or alternatively free-standing to screen off part of the garden.

Clothe rustic trellises with scrambling, informal flowering climbers such as clematis. Several roses have an informal habit and look best when trained up and along rustic poles.

When choosing rustic poles, select those with a uniform thickness of about 10cm (4in), and make sure they are as straight as possible. They are usually sold with the bark attached and for many gardeners this is part of their charm.

CHOICE PLANTS CHECKLIST	
❧ *Clematis chrysocoma*	❧ *Hedera colchica* 'Sulphur Heart' (variegated Persian ivy)
❧ *Hedera canariensis* 'Gloire de Marengo' (variegated Canary Island ivy)	❧ *Jasminum officinale* (common white jasmine)
	❧ *Rosa* 'Zéphirine Drouhin'

GARDEN BOUNDARIES • CHOICES

1

PICKET FENCING

Picket fencing is ideal for bordering front gardens and looks especially good in front of a timber-framed cottage. It is delicate and attractive and when painted white brightens up the garden. However, take care when constructing a picket fence not to make it too high; it is essential that it should not dominate the cottage or look like a fortification. It should also complement the planting, not overpower it. Picket fencing looks especially attractive when an ornamental flowering cherry tree is planted to cascade over it.

It is better to have a narrow border alongside a picket fence than to have a lawn adjoining it. Alternatively, you could dig out a gulley 23cm (9in) wide and 10cm (4in) deep and fill it with shingle.

CHOICE PLANTS CHECKLIST

Deciduous trees to plant alongside a picket fence:
- *Amelanchier lamarckii* (snowy mespilus)
- *Laburnum* x *watereri* 'Vossii' (golden rain tree)
- *Prunus* 'Accolade'
- *Prunus pendula* 'Pendula Rosea' (weeping spring cherry)
- *Prunus padus* 'Watereri' (bird cherry)

2

POST-AND-RAIL FENCING

Post-and-rail fencing is most often used for long boundaries in the country and, traditionally, especially where animals need to be contained. It has a rustic charm and when informal flowering shrubs such as *Ulex europaeus* 'Flore Pleno' (double-flowered gorse) are planted near to the rails the functional but bland nature of this fencing can be harmonized with any garden.

Chestnut paling (sometimes known as split-chestnut paling) is another country-style fence and is cheaper to install. It is formed of split palings secured at the top and bottom with galvanized wire and nailed to stout posts 1.8–2.4m (6–8ft) apart. The fencing is sold in 9m (30ft) lengths and is usually either 90cm (3ft) or 1.8m (6ft) high.

CHOICE PLANTS CHECKLIST

- *Eucryphia* x *nymansensis*
- *Forsythia* x *intermedia* (golden bells)
- *Genista hispanica* (Spanish gorse)
- *Lavatera* 'Rosea' (tree mallow)
- *Rhododendron luteum*
- *Ulex europaeus* 'Flore Pleno' (double-flowered gorse)

❸

WATTLE HURDLES

Wattle hurdles are formed of strips of thin branches woven horizontally around stout poles. Each hurdle is 1.8m (6ft) long and available in several heights. The poles securing the panels should be knocked 60–75cm (24–30in) into the soil. Use galvanized wire to secure the hurdles to the posts.

A semi-formal fence is a better option for areas with strong winds and is made up of interwoven fence panels. These have thin strips of wood woven laterally between several vertical strips. They are sold in 1.8m (6ft) widths, 90cm–1.2m (3–4ft) high, and are secured to square-sectioned posts concreted into the ground. It is essential to paint both types of fence with a plant-friendly preservative to ensure they do not rot.

CHOICE PLANTS CHECKLIST

- *Caryopteris* x *clandonensis* (blue spiraea)
- *Ceratostigma willmottianum* (hardy plumbago)
- *Helichrysum italicum* (curry plant)
- *Ulex europaeus* 'Flore Pleno' (double-flowered gorse)

❹

DRY-STONE WALLS

Dry-stone walls are the traditional boundaries for stone cottages, especially in exposed areas, as they provide extra protection for the plants. They are constructed without mortar, using stones of varying sizes, and are finally capped with large flat stones. If you decide on this type of wall, it is an expensive option: it must be craftsman-built and should harmonize with the cottage. You should only use materials available locally.

An alternative is to have two walls, 23–30cm (9–12in) apart, that lean slightly towards each other. The space between them is filled with compost so that cascading and bushy plants can be planted at the top, as well as trailing types in the sides. You can also plant ferns along the base.

CHOICE PLANTS CHECKLIST

The following is a list of ferns good for planting at the base of a dry-stone wall.
- *Asplenium scolopendrium* (hart's-tongue fern)
- *Matteuccia struthiopteris* (ostrich feather fern)
- *Onoclea sensibilis* (sensitive fern)
- *Polystichum setiferum* (soft shield fern)

33

DECORATIVE FEATURES • CHOICES

1

BEEHIVES AND SKEPS

Even if you do not have the time to devote to keeping bees, old-style skeps or wooden beehives can make attractive ornamental features for the garden. Skeps are traditionally formed of straw, willow or lath and are the oldest form of man-made home for bees. The more familiar stepped wooden hives arrived in the mid-nineteenth century, and were widely adopted because they separated the breeding of the bees from the storage of their honey, allowing the honey to be harvested without destroying the bees' home. Both hives and skeps may be purchased from beekeeping specialists, who will also advise you if you want to take up beekeeping (try a local farm shop or country crafts fair for information).

CHOICE PLANTS CHECKLIST

To attract bees, plant the following:
- *Allium schoenoprasum* (chives)
- *Digitalis purpurea* (foxglove)
- *Iberis umbellata* (candytuft)
- *Mentha spicata* (spearmint)
- *Thymus serpyllum* (wild thyme)

2

DOVES AND DOVECOTES

In earlier centuries doves were kept on many estates in white, elevated constructions called dovecots or dovecotes. These are still often seen on the roofs of outbuildings or attached to walls, though sadly many are now uninhabited.

Nowadays, few gardeners keep doves. Nesting boxes for smaller birds are available in similar shapes to the traditional dovecote, although usually of simpler construction. Attach one to a high pole to give a traditional feel to your garden. If you would like to keep a pair or two of doves, consider your planting first, and choose tough-leaved plants around a dovecote, as doves are notorious leaf rippers. Doves are available from poultry breeders; look in your local press to find likely sources.

CHOICE PLANTS CHECKLIST

- *Crataegus monogyna* (may)
- *Genista hispanica* (Spanish gorse)
- *Ilex aquifolium* (common holly)
- *Mahonia* x *media* 'Charity'
- *Taxus baccata* (English yew)
- *Ulex europaeus* 'Flore Pleno' (double-flowered gorse)

③

SUNDIALS AND ARMILLARY SPHERES

Sundials were known to the Egyptians as early as 1500 BC, while portable sundials were used by the Romans. During the eighteenth century, they became common features in traditional country gardens, where they told the time before clocks became commonplace.

Armillary spheres are astronomical devices that display the relationships between the main circles of the celestial sphere. They also have a long lineage, and have been used as features in large and small gardens since the seventeenth century.

A sundial or a sphere is best put on a plinth to create a focal point in a cottage garden. Surround the base with prostrate and creeping plants for a traditional effect.

CHOICE PLANTS CHECKLIST	
❧ *Calluna vulgaris* (heather)	❧ *Helichrysum italicum*
❧ *Cistus* x *dansereaui*	(curry plant)
(sun rose)	❧ *Lavandula angustifolia*
❧ *Erica carnea* (winter-	'Hidcote' (dwarf lavender)
flowering heather)	❧ *Thymus serpyllum*
	(wild thyme)

④

WELLS AND PUMPS

Wells and pumps, whether functional or decorative, are ideal features for cottage gardens. Only 80 or 90 years ago the unreliability, or non-existence, of a good central water supply meant that most cottages had their own wells. Nowadays a mock well still creates an interesting feature in a garden. They are usually formed of a brick circle with a wood cover, surmounted by winding gear and a handle. If this covers a real but abandoned well, ensure the cover is secure.

Cast-iron pumps are best sited near a wall, where they can be backed and surrounded by low-growing plants. Wells, however, are usually best as freestanding focal points. Around them position plants that will not distract from their outline.

CHOICE PLANTS CHECKLIST	
❧ *Bergenia cordifolia*	❧ *Lavandula angustifolia*
(elephant's ears)	'Hidcote' (dwarf lavender)
❧ *Ceratostigma*	❧ *Nepeta* x *faassenii*
willmottianum	(catmint)
(hardy plumbago)	❧ *Sedum* 'Autumn Joy'
	(ice plant)

OBTAINING COTTAGE GARDEN PLANTS

There are several sources of cottage garden plants, including local garden centres, specialist nurseries, high-street shops, mail order and local plant sales, as well as seeds and cuttings from friends. Often, the range of plants offered by garden centres is limited, whereas specialist nurseries, where they raise their own stock, offer a wider range. It is often much more satisfying, however, to raise your own plants from seed.

The majority of plants are sold in containers. Deciduous trees are often sold bare-rooted for planting during their dormant period. Roses are also sometimes sold this way, their roots covered in moisture-retentive material inside a plastic bag with aeration holes. Bulbs, corms and tubers can be purchased from general sources, although you may need to contact a specialist company for unusual varieties.

RAISING PLANTS FROM SEED
In the past, gardeners would often gather seeds at the end of the growing season for sowing during the following season. This can be a tricky operation, however, and for most people it is more practical to buy fresh seeds each year. If you find that you have too many, you can always share them with a friend.

POINTS TO CONSIDER

When buying container-grown plants there are certain things you should check:
- Compost in containers must be moist but not waterlogged.
- Check if moss is present on the compost's surface; this indicates that the plant has been in the container for too long.
- Check that masses of roots are not protruding out of the container's drainage holes. This indicates that the plant is pot bound and may have suffered.
- Check that the plant is clearly labelled and pests and diseases have not damaged the leaves or stems.
- Check that the plant has not been recently potted up for a quick sale. Loose soil and a plant that leans excessively are clues to this.

PROPAGATING PLANTS
Many herbaceous perennials are easy to raise from seeds sown in a seed bed. When they reach manageable size, move the young plants into a nursery bed until they are well established and then plant them in a border, either in spring or in autumn. Half-hardy annuals are raised from seed sown in gentle warmth in greenhouses or conservatories in late winter or early spring. The seedlings are transferred into seed trays, at the same time being given a slightly lower temperature to encourage sturdy growth.

LAYERING SHRUBS
Layering shrubs is an easy way to increase their numbers *(see opposite)*, but it does take up to a year for a layered stem to develop roots. Layering can be done throughout the year, but spring, late summer and early autumn are the best times. The technique does not involve any expensive equipment – all that is needed is a spade or trowel, secateurs and a strong cane.

BELOW *The bright mauvey-blue herbaceous perennial* Nepeta x faassenii *(catmint) is a must for any cottage garden and works well when planted in a wide drift, mingled with roses.*

TECHNIQUE **PREPARING AND PLANTING BARE-ROOTED ROSES**

1 Remove the protective covering and carefully inspect the plant. Use secateurs to shorten extra long shoots. Additionally, cut off any damaged or thin roots.

2 If the roots are dry, stand them for a couple of days in a large bucket of clean water to ensure that they are full of moisture when planted. Dry roots inhibit the rapid establishment of plants.

3 Dig a hole 20–25cm (8–10in) deep. Form a mound in the base and spread roots over it. Use a board or stick to check that the graft union between the top growth and the roots is 2.5cm (1in) below the surface.

4 Hold the plant upright and gently sprinkle friable soil around and between the roots. Place friable soil over the roots and firm it down gradually, layer by layer, each layer 5cm (2in) thick. Firm planting is essential for the plant's wellbeing.

5 Continue to add layers until the soil around the plant is level with the surrounding area. Use the heel of your boot to firm the final layer. Water the plant, then add a 5cm-(2in-)thick mulch over the soil. The mulch should not touch the stems.

HINTS AND TIPS

Most modern roses have been grafted – the topgrowth of a variety valued for its flowering qualities has been 'spliced' on to the root system of another, stronger-growing rose in order to give the desirable rose better vigour and a faster growth rate. Where the two plants meet is know as the 'graft union'. This looks like a scar, or callus, round the main stem a little way above the roots.

TECHNIQUE **LAYERING SHRUBS**

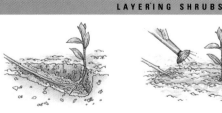

1 Select a low-growing, healthy shoot about one or two years old. Lower it to soil level and make a trench, 7.5–15cm (3–6in) deep, 23–45cm (9–18in) from the shoot's tip.

2 Lower the shoot into the depression and bend its tip upright. Either make a tongued cut at the point of the bend, or cut half-way around the stem and remove part of the bark.

3 Use a strong cane to hold the stem in position and cover with soil; firm and water round it. Tie the end of the stem to the cane.

4 When you see new growth beginning to develop from the shoot's tip, check for roots before you sever the parent stem and plant the new shrub into a nursery bed or a border.

CARE AND MAINTENANCE OF PLANTS

*A*ll plants need careful attention, especially during the first few months after they have . been planted and until they are established and growing strongly. Shrubs, trees and herbaceous perennials take about a year — or at least until after their first winter — to become established. Hardy annuals, half-hardy annuals and biennials live only for a short time, but also need dedicated attention if they are to produce colourful displays.

Trees and shrubs may appear to be self-reliant, but like all other garden plants they benefit from regular attention. During the first spring after they are planted, re-firm any soil that has been loosened by winter frost. Use your heel to ensure that the soil is in close contact with the roots. Then remove all weeds, thoroughly water the soil and place a 7.5–10cm (3–4in) thick mulch over the surface, around the base of the plant.

If it is a tree you are looking after, check that ties securing the trunk to the stake are firm but not strangling it. Also check regularly that none of the branches are misplaced and rubbing against each other. They should be well spread out, forming an attractive shape. Keep an eye out for any diseases. If required, most deciduous trees are best pruned in winter, but for cherry trees and other members of the prunus family wait until the sap starts to rise in spring. Pruning of evergreen trees is best done in spring.

RIGHT *To keep your display looking good, remove faded flowers regularly.*

TECHNIQUE	LOOKING AFTER HARDY ANNUALS

1 Thin seedlings as soon as they are large enough to handle. The spaces to be left between them, usually 10–25cm (4–10in), depend on the ultimate heights and spreads of the plants.

2 Many hardy annuals need to be supported. Insert a twiggy stick between young plants, so that the stems grow up and through them. Trim the stick to the right height with secateurs.

3 Water seedlings and young plants to ensure that their roots do not become dry and damaged. Use oscillating or rotary sprinklers to water the soil thoroughly.

HINTS AND TIPS

Tender shrubs are especially vulnerable to cold wind, particularly when they are young and not well established. This risk can be somewhat diminished by placing a screen made of sacking tied to three stakes on the windward side. Do not totally surround the shrub, but place the screen around half to two-thirds of it. Another type of useful screen is formed of straw sandwiched between two layers of wire netting.

HINTS AND TIPS

❧ In summer, place a few ice cubes on top of the compost in hanging baskets if you are away from home all day and the weather is hot.
❧ If compost in hanging baskets has become very dry, take down the basket and stand its base in a large bowl filled with water for an hour or two before rehanging.
❧ Throughout summer, regularly remove dead flowers from plants in containers to encourage further ones to develop. Also, cut off dead leaves and stems. If left, they look unsightly and encourage diseases.

TECHNIQUE — LOOKING AFTER HARDY BIENNIALS

1 Biennials are sown in V-shaped drills 6–12mm (¼–½in) deep in late spring or early summer. Regularly pull up weeds as they may smother the seedlings.

2 Usually, seedlings are thinned when large enough, leaving just the strongest ones. Alternatively, transfer young plants to nursery beds.

3 In late summer or early autumn, transplant biennials into their flowering positions, spacing them 15–60cm (6–24in) apart, depending on the mature size of the plant.

TECHNIQUE — LOOKING AFTER HERBACEOUS PERENNIALS

1 In early spring, re-firm plants planted during the previous autumn. The soil may have been loosened by frost. Soil must be in close contact with the roots.

2 During spring or early summer, shallowly fork between plants, removing weeds and breaking up the soil surface to enable air and rain to enter.

3 In late spring or early summer, sprinkle a general fertilizer between the plants. Lightly hoe it into the surface, taking care not to damage any of the roots.

4 Soon after, thoroughly but gently water the soil and add a 5–7.5cm (2–3in) layer of well decomposed garden compost between but not touching the plants.

5 Throughout summer, regularly water the soil. This is best done with an oscillating or rotary spray; at each application, thoroughly soak the soil.

6 In late autumn, cut down plants to ground level. In cold areas, leave this job until spring; the stems help to protect the roots from severe frost.

PRUNING COTTAGE GARDEN PLANTS

Pruning is often thought to be a task too complex for an inexperienced gardener to tackle, but both the theory and the practice are logical and simple. Pruning is mainly performed on trees, shrubs and woody climbers, as well as fruit trees and bushes. Its purpose is to encourage the development of flowers and fruits, and to maintain a healthy plant overall.

The timing and technique of pruning differs between types of plants as well as from one species to another. Here we have concentrated on giving details on pruning a wide range of cottage garden trees, shrubs and roses.

PRUNING DECIDUOUS SHRUBS

Climate influences the way in which and when ornamental shrubs need to be pruned. Those in temperate climates can be divided into three main flowering periods that, in turn, influence the way pruning should be tackled.

Spring- and early summer-flowering shrubs have some of the brightest flowers and include *Forsythia* (golden bells), *Philadelphus* (mock orange), *Weigela* and *Ribes* (flowering currants). They develop flowers on the shoots that were produced during the previous year and should be pruned as soon as their flowers fade. It is important to cut out the shoots that produced the flowers, as well as to eliminate any thin and spindly shoots. This will ensure that both light and air are made available to the shrub.

Late summer-flowering shrubs enrich the end of summer and early autumn with colour; their growth and flowering are then curtailed by the onset of cold weather. Examples include *Buddleja davidii* (butterfly bush) and *Ceanothus* 'Gloire de Versailles'. They should be pruned in

TECHNIQUE	PRUNING BUSH ROSES

1 Hard pruning (or low pruning): cut stems back to within three or four buds of the plant's base, leaving stems 13–15cm (5–6in) long. This method is only suitable for newly planted bush roses and weak-growing Hybrid Teas.

2 Moderate pruning (or medium pruning): cut back stems by about half their length. Weaker stems need harder pruning. This method is ideal for Hybrid Teas and Floribundas, and is the one adopted by most rose-growers.

3 Light pruning (or long pruning): cut off the top third of all shoots. This method is used to limit the growth of exceptionally vigorous Hybrid Tea roses, as it does not subsequently encourage the development of strong new shoots.

spring, rather than immediately after their flowers fade. If they are pruned earlier the immediate development of shoots will be encouraged, only for the early shoots subsequently to be killed by frost.

Winter-flowering shrubs and trees are the easiest of all to prune, as they need very little attention. They include *Hamamelis* (witch hazel), *Cornus mas* (cornelian cherry) and *Chimonanthus praecox* (wintersweet). Pruning is very straightforward: in spring, cut out any damaged, crossing or diseased shoots.

PRUNING EVERGREEN SHRUBS

Evergreens are continuously clothed in leaves, although throughout the year some will fall off while new ones take their place. Established shrubs need little pruning, other than cutting out weak, straggly and diseased shoots in spring. In cold areas, never attempt this process until all risk of frost has passed. If the shrub flowers in spring, it is best to delay pruning until the flowers have completely faded. This applies to evergreen flowering shrubs such as *Berberis darwinii* and *Berberis* x *stenophylla*.

PRUNING BUSH ROSES

Pruning is a yearly job with Hybrid Tea (large-flowered bush roses) and Floribunda roses (cluster-flowered roses). These are popular in gardens, although in a cottage garden

ABOVE *Bush roses need careful pruning to produce a fine display. The tree in this cottage-garden path has been pruned to create a 'standard' to match the rose bushes in the beds.*

context these plants are relatively new introductions. Every rose expert has a different opinion about the correct time to prune these roses, but the consensus is as follows: established roses, as well as autumn- and winter-planted ones, are best pruned in early spring, just as growth begins but before any leaves appear. Bush roses planted in spring, on the other hand, should ideally be pruned as soon as they have been planted.

To prevent bushes being rocked in the soil by strong winter winds, cut back any long shoots during early winter. Then, in spring, carry out the appropriate level of pruning for your particular bush rose. There are three degrees of pruning – hard, moderate and light. Each of these has a different influence on subsequent growth and they are described in the technique panel, 'Pruning Bush Roses' *(see opposite).*

FLOWERS FOR COTTAGE GARDENS

Informal borders and beds drenched in colour throughout summer are prime features of cottage gardens. These may be created with a medley of plants, including herbaceous perennials, summer-flowering bulbs, half-hardy annuals and hardy annuals. As well as brightening the garden, the flowers of many of the hardy annuals and herbaceous perennials can be cut for use in flower arrangements. Some of them can also be dried.

Hardy annuals, unlike herbaceous perennials, can be changed each year, and this encourages cottage gardeners to be more adventurous and experimental with their overall planting schemes. New varieties are also introduced annually, so a browse through a seed catalogue can be a real adventure during dull winter months, and will excite the imagination ready for the next planting time.

CREATING A MEDLEY

Cottage gardens readily welcome mixtures of all types of plants. Shrubs and trees offer a degree of permanency around which more ephemeral plants can be placed. Beware when trying to grow plants under a canopy of leaves from trees, however, as the soil will be dry, shaded and deprived of nutrients. Herbaceous perennials, such as

---

PROJECT   **PLANTING HERBACEOUS BORDERS**

1 Use scaled paper to plot the border's size and shape. Mark the individual planting areas, making them irregular and overlapping rather than regimented.

2 Rake the border so that it is level or has a gentle slope. Then, transfer the plan to the border, using either a pointed stick or a thin line of sharp sand.

3 Place the plants in position. When three plants of each species are used, form them into irregular triangles. Avoid creating straight lines of plants.

4 When the design is right, use a trowel to set each plant in position. Ensure that the planting hole is deep enough to prevent roots being constricted and twisted.

5 Draw soil around the roots and firm it with your hands. When planting is complete, level the soil and thoroughly but gently water the area. Label the plants.

STAR PLANTS

These perennials provide flowers and seedheads for drying.

- *Acanthus spinosus* (bear's breeches)
- *Anaphalis triplinervis* (life everlasting)
- *Dictamnus albus* (burning bush)
- *Gypsophila paniculata* (baby's breath)
- *Papaver orientale* (Oriental poppy)
- *Stachys byzantina* (lamb's ear)

TECHNIQUE — SUPPORTING HERBACEOUS PERENNIALS

1 Insert twiggy sticks around the plants while they are still young. Shoots will grow up and through the sticks which will help support them as they develop.

2 Insert three stout stakes around a plant, and then encircle the stakes with green string. The plant will eventually hide the support as it grows up and through it.

3 Insert proprietary, curved, metal supports around the plant. Again, this type of support will eventually be hidden by the developing plant.

STAR PLANTS

The following plants provide excellent cut flowers for use in the home.

Herbaceous perennials
- *Achillea* 'Coronation Gold' (fern-leaf yarrow)
- *Aconitum napellus* (monkshood)
- *Agapanthus praecox* (African lily)
- *Coreopsis verticillata* (tickseed)
- *Leucanthemum x superbum* (shasta daisy)
- *Lysimachia punctata* (yellow loosestrife)
- *Phlox paniculata*
- *Solidago* 'Crown of Rays' (golden rod)

Annuals
- *Antirrhinum majus* (snapdragon)
- *Calendula officinalis* (pot marigold)
- *Gypsophila elegans* (baby's breath)
- *Lathyrus odoratus* (sweet pea)
- *Nigella damascena* (love-in-a-mist)

Lilium auratum (golden-rayed lily) is particularly attractive as well as easy to grow. Cottage gardens benefit from tall plants being peppered among lower-growing ones, as this will create an interesting attraction and variation of height. You should also take into account, when planning your planting scheme, that most cottage gardens will be viewed from several angles. Avoid single-colour themes, as these can suppress the freedom of colour that is one of the key features of an authentic cottage garden.

BELOW *Unusual colour combinations can be very striking. Don't be afraid to experiment freely with interesting new varieties of your favourite plants.*

achillea and sedum, are better than hardy annuals at withstanding such dry conditions. Herbaceous perennials can last for up to five years before being lifted, divided and replanted to sustain their strength.

Newly planted borders often have gaps and annuals and bulbs are especially good for filling these up. Lilies, for example, bring colour and distinctive shapes to a border.

FRAGRANT LAWNS, PATHS AND SEATS

*S*cented borders may be the hallmark of cottage gardens, but there is no reason why lawns and paths should also not be fragrant. Clearly, the range of suitable plants is not as wide as that for border plants – nevertheless such features have great appeal and never fail to give pleasure. In addition to fragrant lawns, scented seats are attractive when positioned as focal points at the ends of paths or as part of a romantic arbour.

Grass – with its resilience and ease of maintenance – is the plant normally used to create lawns. It is also the best surface when a hardwearing area is needed for children and dogs to play on. Lawns do not *have* to be made of grass, however. For a fragrant lawn, path or seat try using chamomile or thyme instead.

CHAMOMILE LAWNS

These lawns were popular in Elizabethan times and were often used to create bowling areas. It was probably on a lawn like this that Sir Francis Drake was playing when the Spanish Armada was sighted in the English Channel in 1588. Chamomile (*Chamaemelum nobile*) is a prostrate, mat-forming herbaceous perennial. It has finely dissected mid-green leaves that emit a fruity scent when bruised. The non-flowering form 'Treneague' is ideal for forming a lawn. Walking on a chamomile lawn crushes the foliage and releases the fragrance, but do this sparingly, as the plant is not as tough as grass.

Weeds can be a problem, and for this reason it is best to tackle them before you plant a chamomile lawn. Dig the soil thoroughly during one winter, and in the following 12 months leave the soil bare but regularly hoe off annual weeds and dig up perennial ones. In the second winter, again dig the soil but leave the surface level rough, so that wind, rain and frost can break down the surface by spring.

POINTS TO CONSIDER

🍃 Fragrant seats can also be a unique addition to a garden. Grass seats, in which a grassy, flat-topped mound is used as a bench, work well, but try planting thyme or chamomile instead. Regular watering is essential, as the raised area soon becomes dry. If the scented bench is long, intersperse the plants with small paving slabs or slatted wooden seats about 45cm (18in) square. The latter are warmer and more comfortable, but will eventually decay and will need to be replaced with new ones.

PROJECT — PLANTING A CHAMOMILE LAWN

1 In late spring or early summer, shuffle over the soil with your feet to firm it. Then, rake it level and lightly but thoroughly water the entire area.

2 Allow the surface to dry. Space the plants 15–20cm (6–8in) apart in staggered rows. Firm the soil around their roots and carefully level the area.

3 Lightly but thoroughly water the lawn to settle the roots in the soil. When the plants have started to form a 'carpet', use sharp hedging shears to trim them.

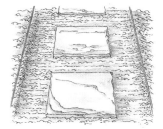

1 During winter, mark the path's width and thoroughly dig the area to remove perennial weeds. Leave the surface level but rough to allow wind, rain and frost to break down the surface.

2 In spring, uniformly firm the surface by shuffling over it; then rake the area level. Next, place the stepping stones in position. Check that their spacings will suit everyone in the family.

3 Position the stones so that their surfaces are about 12mm (½in) above the soil's surface. Plant the thymes 23–30cm (9–12in) apart. Firm soil around them and thoroughly water the entire area.

All that is then needed is for you to firm the surface with your feet and rake it level. Do not use a lawn roller at this stage as it consolidates the surface unevenly.

Plant a chamomile lawn in late spring or early summer, spacing plants 15–20 cm (6–8in) apart. The lawn will need rolling once the plants start to grow, as this will firm them into the soil. It takes about a year for the lawn to be ready. During this time you must remove weeds regularly, taking care not to loosen chamomile roots.

THYME PATHS

These are colourful, fragrant and unusual. *Thymus serpyllum* (wild thyme) is one of the best thymes to use. This is a carpet-forming evergreen plant with grey-green leaves that exude a rich scent. It has flowers throughout much of summer in red through pink to white. Established plants have a 45–60cm (18–24in) spread, but to ensure quick coverage they can be planted 23–30cm (9–12in) apart.

Thyme paths on their own are not robust enough for daily traffic, but you can position stepping stones to make it more practical. Put these stones in place before you start. They will help to keep the path looking its best.

RIGHT *Once your fragrant thyme path is established it will have the extra attraction of copious flowers in summer, making it a delight to walk through the garden.*

FRUIT IN COTTAGE GARDENS

*T*he integration of fruit, as well as vegetables and herbs, with ornamental plants sets cottage gardens apart from other styles of garden. The range of fruits is wide, from tree types such as apples, pears and plums to bush fruits such as gooseberries and blackcurrants. Also, there are cane fruits such as raspberries and loganberries, and few cottage gardens would be complete without strawberries, grown either in containers or special beds.

There can be few better experiences in a garden than picking fresh fruit. It takes tree fruits several years to produce large crops, but if you plant soft fruits you will soon be gathering their produce from your garden.

TREE FRUITS

Growing these in cottage gardens gives gardeners the opportunity to plant interesting varieties that are not grown commercially. In earlier cottage gardens, apples were mainly grown as trees, but in small gardens they may be trained as espaliers or cordons against a sunny wall or alongside a row of supporting wires. Dwarfing rootstocks now enable apples to be grown in very small gardens, as well as in large pots on a patio. Recommended dessert varieties include 'Ashmead Kernel', which has a crisp flesh. Pick it in autumn and it will be ready to use in winter to early spring. 'Egremont Russet' has a superb flavour and should be picked in late summer ready for use in autumn. 'Ellison's Orange' is juicy and has a rich aroma

and aniseed flavour. Pick it in early autumn and it will be ready to eat in mid-autumn.

Pears are more difficult to grow than apples. Dessert pears need a sunnier position, and shelter from cold wind. They flower earlier and are more prone to damage from late frosts. They survive in heavy soil but are susceptible to drought. The range of varieties is more limited than with apples and in cottage gardens it is best to plant dessert varieties rather than cooking types. 'Doyenne du Comice' has a superb flavour. Pick it in the middle of autumn for use in late autumn and early winter. 'Winter Nelis' has a good keeping quality. It should be picked in mid-autumn and can be used from late autumn to midwinter.

SOFT FRUITS

Growing strawberries in barrels was popular in 'old' cottage gardens *(see right above)*. They can also be grown in strawberry planters, as well as in ornamental pots. Raspberries are also popular. There are two types: summer-

TECHNIQUE	PICKING AND STORING PEARS

   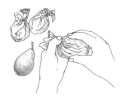

1 Pick pears individually, testing each fruit. Hold the fruit in the palm of your hand and at the same time gently lift and twist. If the stalk parts from the branch, the fruit is ready to be picked.

2 If left on the tree too long, early pear varieties can become mealy and soft. They can be harvested by using sharp scissors to cut the stalk close to the branch. Take care not to bruise the fruit.

3 Store pears by placing them on slatted trays in a cool, frost-proof, dark and airy shed or cellar. Check for any decay regularly to ensure that a bad pear does not spoil the rest of the fruit.

4 Alternatively, wrap fruits individually; this helps to prevent them drying out. Unfortunately, it also prevents early signs of decay in the fruits being readily seen so may mean that it spreads.

PLANTING A STRAWBERRY BARREL

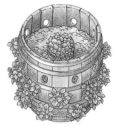

1 Select a strong barrel and thoroughly clean it. Turn it upside down and drill several 2.5cm (1in) wide holes in the base to ensure good drainage. Use a chisel or coarse, round file to clean out the holes.

2 Stand the barrel upright and drill several 5–6.5cm (2–2½in) wide holes, about 20cm (8in) apart, between each metal band. Ensure that each hole is drilled in the middle of one stave, and not across two.

3 Place on three bricks and fill the base with coarse drainage material. Stand a wire-netting tube in the centre and fill with rubble. Fill the barrel with compost and plant in the sides and top.

STAR PLANTS

- *Ficus carica* (fig)
- *Fragaria* x *ananassa* (strawberry)
- *Malus domestica* (apple)
- *Prunus avium* (cherry)
- *Prunus domestica* (plum)
- *Prunus persica* (peach)
- *Pyrus communis* (pear)
- *Ribes nigrum* (blackcurrant)
- *Ribes rubrum* (redcurrant)
- *Ribes uva-crispa* (gooseberry)
- *Rubus fruticosus* (blackberry)
- *Rubus idaeus* (raspberry)

fruiting and autumn-fruiting. Summer-fruiting ones yield much more fruit. They need a position in full sun, shelter from cold winds, a fertile, moisture-retentive soil and support. Prune fruited canes to ground level – for summer types do this as soon as fruits have been picked, for autumn types do it in late winter.

OTHER FRUITS

Blackcurrants, redcurrants and gooseberries are popular bush fruits that are easy to grow. Blackcurrant bushes have many shoots rising from ground level, while both red-currants and gooseberries grow on short stems known as 'legs'. Blackcurrants tolerate poor drainage better than the other fruits, and a position either in full sun or light shade is suitable for them all.

ABOVE To save space, and to make the fruit easily accessible, apple trees are sometimes trained over a number of years as 'espaliers' along a set of parallel wires.

VEGETABLES IN COTTAGE GARDENS

*V**egetables are fundamental to a cottage garden, where they provide fresh food as well as looking decorative. Some vegetables, such as globe artichokes and runner beans, which can be grown on tepees, can be used in flower borders as well as in vegetable areas. The informality of a cottage garden sometimes gives the mistaken impression that vegetable seeds have been randomly scattered; instead they are normally sown in drills and in rows so that weeding and general cultivation are made easier for the gardener.*

Always grow vegetables in moderately fertile, well-drained but moisture-retentive soil in an open, sunny position away from overhanging trees that might drip water over them. A slight slope facing the sun encourages crops to mature early. Some plants, such as melons, cucumbers and tomatoes, are susceptible to cold weather and are therefore best grown in growing-bags and other containers on a sunny, sheltered patio or terrace.

ROTATING CROPS

Some crops, such as rhubarb and asparagus, are left in one position for many years, but the majority need yearly rotation from one part of the garden to another. This prevents a build-up of pests and diseases that affect specific vegetables. Vegetables can be placed in three groups, as follows. Each year, the crops should be rotated so each group grows in a different place. Root crops include beetroot, carrots,

---

PROJECT	MAKING A RUNNER BEAN TEPEE

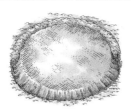

1 Mark out a circle 1.5m (5ft) in diameter and dig out a trench 10cm (4in) deep. Level the ground and lay out a geotextile membrane, pushing the extra material into the trench and covering it with soil.

2 Place some tall bamboo poles around the circle roughly 60cm (24in) apart, leaving a gap for the tepee entrance. Push the bamboos in at an angle, at least 30cm (12in) into the ground or until they feel firm.

3 Tie the bamboos together in the middle with garden twine, 15cm (6in) below the top of the poles. Plant a runner bean plant on the outside of each of the poles, and water in well.

4 Sow a circle of carrot seeds around the outside of the runner beans, leaving the entrance to the tepee clear. The carrots will protect the beans from pests.

5 To support the beans further, tie rows of garden string around the circle of bamboos at regular intervals, leaving the entrance clear.

6 Ensure that the beans twine around the poles rather than dangling in mid-air. Add a couple of small paving stones to give dry access to the tepee during showers.

TECHNIQUE   **SOWING VEGETABLE SEEDS**

 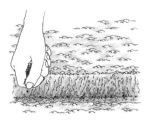

1   Form V-shaped drills with a draw hoe. Use a garden line to ensure the row is straight. If the row is long, stand on the line to prevent it being moved sideways when the drill is being formed.

2   Sow seeds evenly and thinly in the base of the drill. Ensure seeds are spaced out and not touching; congested seeds have to compete for light, air, moisture and nutrients. This also saves seeds.

3   Sow some seeds, such as parsnips, in small groups spaced 15cm (6in) apart along the drill's base. After germination, remove the weakest seedlings, leaving only the strongest.

4   Thin the seedlings as soon as they are large enough to handle. Re-firm the soil around the remaining seedlings and thoroughly but gently water them. Pick up and remove any unwanted seedlings.

5   Flat-bottomed trenches for sowing garden peas are formed with a draw hoe or spade. Sow peas in three rows, 7.5cm (3in) apart; space the seeds a similar distance apart.

STAR PLANTS

- *Allium cepa* (onion)
- *Asparagus officinalis* (asparagus)
- *Brassica oleracea* (Botrytis group, cauliflower)
- *Cynara scolymus* (globe artichoke)
- *Daucus carota* (carrot)
- *Lactuca sativa* (lettuce)
- *Lycopersicon esculentum* (tomato)
- *Phaseolus coccineus* (runner bean)

HINTS AND TIPS

When sowing vegetable seeds, the depths of the V-shaped drills will vary, depending on the vegetable.
- 12mm (½in): chicory, endive, leeks, lettuce, onions, salsify
- 12–18mm (½–¾in): asparagus, carrots, kohl rabi, marrows, parsnips, radishes, spinach, swedes, turnips
- 18–25mm (¾–1in): broccoli, Brussels sprouts, cabbages and cauliflower
- 25mm (1in): beetroot, sweetcorn
- 5cm (2in): garden peas, beans – French, runner, haricot and soya
- 7.5cm (3in): broad beans
- 15cm (6in): Jerusalem artichokes and potatoes

Jerusalem artichokes, parsnips, potatoes, salsify and scorzonera. A couple of weeks before sowing or planting these vegetables, rake in a general fertilizer. Brassicas include broccoli, Brussels sprouts, cabbage, cauliflowers, kale, kohl rabi, radishes and swedes. Before planting these, dig the soil in early winter and mix in well-decomposed manure or compost. Dust the soil with lime in late winter and rake in a general fertilizer before sowing. The final group is more general, and includes aubergines, beans, capsicums, celery, celeriac, leeks, lettuce, marrows, onions, peas, spinach, sweetcorn and tomatoes. For these, dig the soil in early winter and mix in well-decomposed manure or garden compost. If the soil is acidic, apply lime in late winter and rake in a general fertilizer prior to sowing or planting.

HERBS IN COTTAGE GARDENS

*I*n the past, herbs were often used to mask incipient decay in food, and many were also thought to have a medicinal value. These ranged from wound herbs such as daisies, mignonette and snowdrops to those used to control pain and allay fevers. There were others with more homely uses. To take just one example, lady's bedstraw, with its honey-fragrant flowers and leaves, was dried and used to stuff mattresses, and in some countries was also thought to have medicinal properties that helped women in childbirth.

Even without a large garden the joy of growing herbs is available to everyone. A few pots on a patio, a windowbox or spaces left in natural stone paving can become homes for herbs. Some, such as angelica and fennel, are large and dominant and best grown in borders. Rosemary, an evergreen and aromatic shrub, is also ideal for a border or a hedge. For windowboxes and troughs, use small, bushy herbs such as mint (in pots), chives and thyme. Try putting troughs at the edges of balconies or along the sides of patios. Growing-bags are ideal for patios or balconies, and perfect for invasive plants such as mints. Use new or recycled bags, and add a dusting of general fertilizer before planting. Planters have cupped holes at their sides into which small herbs can be planted. Large tubs are ideal for shrub-like herbs such as rosemary and bay. For a decorative planting you can use an old cartwheel, positioning plants between the spokes.

USES OF HERBS

Herbs are extremely versatile. In the kitchen, chives will spice up a potato salad, and flowers from different herbs can not only add decoration to salads but are also edible. As herbal medicine is again increasing in popularity, your herb garden may also help keep your family healthy. *Borago officinalis* (borage), for example, has been used as a cold and flu remedy, as well as a cure for coughs. Do not use your herbs medicinally, however, without expert advice.

Several herbs have leaves that can be used to create soothing herbal teas and cold drinks. *Melissa officinalis* (balm), for example, is excellent for flavouring iced drinks and fruit salads. Mint can be used in a similar way to produce a distinctively flavoured drink.

Many flowering and foliage herbs are ideal for cutting to display indoors. Their sweet, refreshing fragrances permeate the whole house. When cutting the stems of

TECHNIQUE **DRYING HERBS IN YOUR KITCHEN**

1 Few sights are more attractive in a cottage-garden kitchen than bunches of herbs hanging from ceiling beams. Herbs can be dried in a gently warmed oven, but the best method is to hang them up.

2 Pick shoots and leaves while they are still young and before the plant begins to develop flowers. Cut them in the morning on a warm, dry day before the sun is at its hottest.

3 Tie the herbs in small bunches and hang them up a well ventilated, dry and fairly warm room. Slow drying is essential, and usually this takes around 5–12 days.

1   Check that drainage holes in the base of the container are clear, then place it in position ready for planting. Put pieces of broken clay pots over the drainage holes, then 2.5–3.5cm (1–1½in) of pea shingle.

2   Select healthy plants of your favourite herbs. Leave them in their pots and water thoroughly. Then place in the trough, with trailing plants at the front and bushy plants at the centre.

3   To keep the compost moist and cool – especially if the herbs will be in full sun all day – pack moist peat around the pots. If individual plants become dominant, exchange them for others.

STAR PLANTS

- *Allium schoenoprasum* (chives)
- *Angelica archangelica* (angelica)
- *Borago officinalis* (borage)
- *Carum carvi* (caraway)
- *Foeniculum vulgare* (fennel)
- *Melissa officinalis* (balm)
- *Mentha spicata* (spearmint)
- *Ocimum basilicum* (basil)
- *Rosmarinus officinalis* (rosemary)
- *Salvia officinalis* (sage)
- *Thymus vulgaris* (common thyme)

herbs, ensure that the cut is angled. This allows water to enter stems even when they are in the base of a vase. Stand them in fresh, clean water and place in a cool room for 24 hours. Then, remove the plants and recut the stems to ensure that there is not an airlock in them. The choice of herbs for floral displays indoors is wide and includes sage, borage, rosemary and thyme. For extra colour when using sage, add a few sprigs of the purple-leaved form. Trailing plants help to unify the display. Seed heads can also introduce further interest.

ABOVE *Some herbs, such as mint, are invasive and can take over the garden if planted without care. They are best grown in a pot or other container like this old bucket.*

WATER FEATURES

*I*nformality is essential in water features for cottage gardens. Irregularly shaped ponds, perhaps with a kidney outline, can be integrated into casual gardens more easily and naturally than square, rectangular or even round ones. Wildlife ponds, surrounded in part by moisture-retentive soil that allows bog plants to be grown, are even easier to harmonize with the cottage-garden style. In addition to ponds, ornamental water features such as wells and cast-iron water pumps evoke the atmosphere of an earlier age.

Ponds are the most obvious and straightforward of water features. They can be created from a range of materials, including concrete and moulded liners (sometimes called rigid liners), either at ground level or raised up to 45cm (18in) high. However, flexible liners (also known as pool liners) offer the easiest way to create an informal pond.

BOG GARDENS AND WILDLIFE PONDS

These create added interest in cottage gardens and extend the range of plants that can be grown. They encourage the presence of wildlife, from frogs and toads to birds and insects. First, create the pond in the normal way, allowing for a bog-garden area beside it. At the edge of the pond,

| PROJECT | CREATING AN ORNAMENTAL WELL FEATURE |

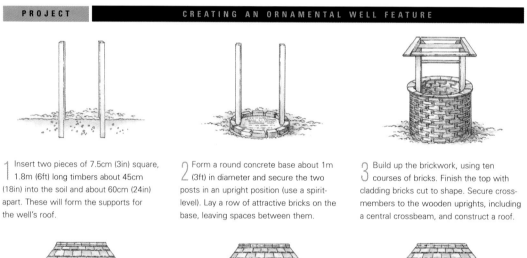

1 Insert two pieces of 7.5cm (3in) square, 1.8m (6ft) long timbers about 45cm (18in) into the soil and about 60cm (24in) apart. These will form the supports for the well's roof.

2 Form a round concrete base about 1m (3ft) in diameter and secure the two posts in an upright position (use a spirit-level). Lay a row of attractive bricks on the base, leaving spaces between them.

3 Build up the brickwork, using ten courses of bricks. Finish the top with cladding bricks cut to shape. Secure cross-members to the wooden uprights, including a central crossbeam, and construct a roof.

4 Clad the roof in roofing tiles, placing a row of ridging tiles along the top. Add a rope to the beam to give the impression that there is a bucket on the end of it.

5 If a border exists around the well, you can put plants directly into the soil. Choose informal plants – a wide range is suggested in the box above right.

6 If you decide to put stone paving around your well, you can place low-growing plants such as *Thymus serpyllum* (wild thyme) in the cracks between the slabs.

STAR PLANTS

Plants to position around the base of an ornamental well.

- *Alchemilla mollis* (lady's mantle)
- *Caryopteris* x *clandonensis* (blue spiraea)
- *Ceratostigma willmottianum* (hardy plumbago)
- *Erica carnea* (winter-flowering heather)
- *Fuchsia magellanica* (lady's eardrops)
- *Lavandula angustifolia* 'Hidcote' (lavender)
- *Limnanthes douglasii* (poached egg plant)
- *Matteuccia struthiopteris* (ostrich feather fern)
- *Nepeta* x *faassenii* (catmint)
- *Onoclea sensibilis* (sensitive fern)
- *Stachys byzantina* (lamb's ear)
- *Thymus serpyllum* (wild thyme)

ABOVE *Plants such as hostas and ferns are ideal companions for water features, giving the surrounding area a lush appearance with their vibrant, attractive foliage.*

leave a few spaces for little ramps that will enable mammals such as voles and shrews to escape from the water if they fall in. Ramps can be made from small planks of wood, waterproofed and propped along the pond's edges.

The bog garden is then formed from a thin, plastic liner (with holes made in its base to enable excess water to drain away), covered with a layer of soil. Hide the edges of the liner with large pebbles to make an informal edge, as well as to prevent the plastic liner being exposed to sunlight, which will cause it to deteriorate. Plant astilbes and other moisture-loving perennials close to the pebbles to cloak their outline. The distinctive ferns *Matteuccia struthiopteris* (ostrich feather fern) and *Onoclea sensibilis* (sensitive fern) are also suitable for this purpose. When looking after a wildlife pond – or any other water feature that may be home to fish, amphibians or mammals – never use chemical sprays to control pests, diseases or weeds in surrounding borders.

Birds play a role in a bog garden, especially if it is near a wild garden. Although they often tear at plants, they do eat grubs and insects. By positioning bird-feeders near a bog garden, many birds can be encouraged into the area.

ORNAMENTAL FEATURES

Splashing water never fails to create vibrancy in gardens and can be introduced by installing a small, ornamental water feature such as a bubble fountain or a spouting gargoyle. Most of these water features have no practical function, other than to excite the eye and ear. They need a small electrical or solar-powered water pump to recycle the water. A few include pipes that conduct water from gutters into water butts, with functional but ornamental water pumps raising the water when needed. These can be surrounded by moisture-loving plants for added interest and decoration.

Although not strictly a water feature, an ornamental well can give a garden the suggestion of water, and looks good positioned at the junction of a path or alongside a rustic patio, particularly when surrounded by plants. They are not hard to make, and require only basic bricklaying and woodworking skills *(see opposite)*.

GRASS IN COTTAGE GARDENS

*L*awns and grass paths are fundamental aspects of most gardens. They have a relaxing *colour, and create a non-dominant background for other, more eye-catching plants. They also help to unify gardens, inexpensively linking one part with another. Apart from forming a traditional lawn, grass can also be used in other ways — for example, grass combines well with spring-flowering bulbs in alpine meadows. There are also many ornamental grasses that look attractive when planted in and among more conventional border plants.*

The relaxed nature of a cottage garden creates superb opportunities for using grass in different ways. As well as traditional lawns and paths, it can be used to create grass steps, which are especially attractive in informal areas. Broad, gently sloping steps, with thick logs used as risers and daffodils bursting with colour along their edges, create an exciting feature. Grassy knolls, elevated and sited as vantage points in a wild garden, allow a bird's-eye view of plants. A rustic bench will add to this effect. Additionally, a grassy 'lay-by' alongside a path can be given a permanent

STAR PLANTS

The following beautiful ornamental grasses are superb when planted in a cottage garden.

- *Coix lacryma-jobi* (Job's tears)
- *Festuca glauca* (blue fescue)
- *Holcus mollis* 'Albovariegatus'
- *Miscanthus sinensis* 'Variegatus'
- *Pennisetum villosum* (feather grass)
- *Phalaris arundinaceae* var. *picta* (gardeners' garters)

garden seat made from logs or stone. In wild gardens, plants of many types can grown in grass which is not mown regularly — a smothering of miniature bulbs gives a great show in spring. Ornamental grasses placed in a border must be left to grow naturally — never be tempted to cut them.

PLANTING BULBS IN GRASS

One of the most effective and simple ways of using grass to its fullest effect in a cottage garden is to combine it with bulbs. Daffodils look spectacular when planted in large drifts in areas towards the outer edges of an informally shaped lawn, while smaller bulbs or corms such as *Colchicum* 'Waterlily' (autumn crocus) are especially attractive when grown under trees.

Plant daffodils in late summer or early autumn, as soon as the bulbs are available. First, cut the grass and then scatter the bulbs randomly on the surface. This usually creates a more natural-looking arrangement than positioning each bulb individually. To create a dominant display,

LEFT *A flowering meadow is one of the most attractive sights in the countryside, and it is quite easy to recreate the effect in your cottage garden using bulbs or wildflowers.*

TECHNIQUE   **LAYING TURF**

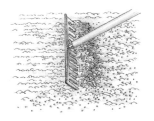

1 Dig the soil over and weed thoroughly. Systematically shuffle over the surface to firm it evenly. Do not use a roller. Then dust the soil with a general fertilizer.

2 Use a metal rake to work the fertilizer into the soil and to level the surface. Prepare an area slightly larger than the area that will eventually be needed for the lawn.

3 Stretch a garden line along the longest side. Ensure that the line is straight and lay a line of turfs, butting the end of each turf right up to its neighbour.

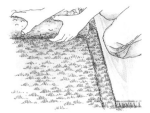

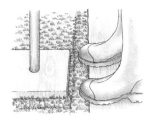

4 Place a board about 23cm (9in) wide and 1.8m (6ft) long on the turfs and lay the next row. Ensure that the turfs are close together and that the joints are staggered.

5 Stand on the board and systematically use a large, heavy firmer to press the turfs into the soil, so that both are in close contact with one another.

6 Trickle fine compost between the joints, ensuring that it is well worked into any cracks that may remain. Then, use a twig broom to brush over the surface lightly.

however, do not space them more than 10cm (4in) apart. When you are happy with their positions, use either a trowel or a bulb-planting tool to plant them. The bulb-planter takes out a core of soil and grass, leaving a hole into which a single bulb can be placed. The depth of the hole should be about three times the depth of the bulb.

Ensure that the base of the bulb rests firmly on the soil in the base of the planting hole, and then replace the plug of turf (having first removed some soil from the plug's base to prevent it crushing the bulb and standing above the level of the surrounding grass). Firm into position, and gently but thoroughly water the whole area. Do not cut the grass until the bulbs have finished flowering and the foliage has completely died down. It is a good idea to use canes and

string to mark off the planted area during winter so that the tiny new shoots are not trodden on. When they are visible above the turf the markers can be removed.

When planting small bulbs (or corms) over a large area, either use a trowel or press a metal rod into the soil to about 7.5cm (3in) deep. Then insert the bulb, and cover it with friable soil. When planting small pockets of bulbs in turf, use a garden spade to remove the turf to a depth of 7.5cm (3in). Put the bulbs in position, remove some of the soil from the base of the turf and replace it. It is also possible to use an edging-iron to cut lines in the lawn's surface, about 30cm (12in) apart, and for the turf to be rolled back to enable small bulbs to be planted. Then replace and firm the turf, and thoroughly water the area.

ORNAMENTAL TREES FOR COTTAGE GARDENS

*F*ew sights are as attractive in a cottage garden as a large, spreading, spring-flowering ornamental cherry tree in full flower and surrounded by golden daffodils. As well as introducing colour into a garden, flowering trees create a permanent structure, around which other plants can be used creatively. Trees need space, however, so before purchasing a new one that appeals to you check that its branches will not ultimately extend over a neighbour's garden, where they might be radically cut back, destroying the natural symmetry of the tree.

There are many flowering trees that will give colour to a cottage garden. The range includes spring-, summer- and winter-flowering examples. During mid-spring, *Amelanchier lamarckii* (snowy mespilus) produces masses of pure white star-shaped flowers. It is such a beautiful tree that most visitors to your garden will walk over to look at it more closely, so position it where it is close to a path's edge, rather than at the back of the border where it will be less accessible – otherwise you risk having your plants trampled. Underplant it with large, golden-yellow, trumpet-shaped daffodils for the best effect. Additionally, the tree has stunning foliage in autumn.

For a beautiful mid- and late spring display, choose the deciduous *Magnolia stellata* (star magnolia), which bears

large, white flowers, up to 10cm (4in) wide. *Prunus* 'Accolade', with its deep blush-pink flowers, becomes a bright colour focus in early and mid-spring.

As spring passes into early summer, there are even more flowering trees to choose from. One that is sure to capture anyone's attention is the stunning *Laburnum* x *watereri* 'Vossii' (golden rain tree). This bears large pendulous clusters of golden-yellow flowers.

With the onset of winter, flowering trees become a focus, and few are better than *Hamamelis mollis* (Chinese witch hazel). It bears golden-yellow spider-like flowers on naked branches from early to mid-winter and is an ideal companion for the golden variegated evergreen shrub *Euonymus japonicus* 'Duc d' Anjou'. This combination will bring brightness into the garden at the dullest time of year.

LEFT *The blossom of ornamental* Prunus *(cherries) can look spectacular in spring, especially when offset by clumps or drifts of bright yellow daffodils.*

PROJECT   **PLANTING A CLIMBING ROSE THROUGH AN OLD TREE**

1 Dig a hole 45–60cm (12–24in) square and deep, and 60cm (24in) from the trunk of the tree. Attach some wire to the tree to support the rose while it is growing.

2 Check that water drains from the hole's base, then replace the old soil with fertile soil. Firm the soil down.

3 Dig a hole to accommodate the roots, so that the dark soil mark on the stem lies slightly deeper than before. Firm the soil in layers around and over the roots.

4 Insert a 1.8m (6ft) long stout cane near to the roots and at an angle so that it meets the trunk. Tie the top to the trunk.

5 Very gently, angle the shoots of the rose and tie them to the cane. Take care not to break the shoots.

6 Regularly water the soil until the rose's roots are established and the shoots are growing strongly towards and up the trunk.

DIFFERENT USES FOR TREES

Trees can be used to create distant focal points, or be positioned within a flower border with a medley of flowering plants around them. They also look beautiful with flowering climbers, such as clematis or roses, growing up and over them *(see above)*.

Trees can be planted so that their branches cascade over picket fences and stone walls, thus softening the boundaries. They also make good central feature within a garden, or in the middle of a lawn. Circular seats can be constructed around a tree, or the lawn area used as a picnic spot to make use of the shade from the branches. Wide circular brick paths can be laid under and around them, but if you decide to make a path, be careful not to damage any roots that are near the surface.

Many old pictures of cottage gardens show a young child on a swing suspended from a branch. However idyllic this may appear, do not copy it in your garden – few trees make a safe site for a swing. In addition, the branch structure of an ornamental tree takes many years to form and if a limb breaks off the tree may become lop-sided and ugly.

Fixing wooden nesting-boxes to trees encourages the presence of birds. Remember, however, that some birds peck at blossom on ornamental trees, while in an orchard or fruit garden finches will soon devastate buds. This can often cause shoots to become 'blind', while the complete destruction of fruit buds has obvious consequences. It is possible to protect bush fruits and both cordon and espalier trees with netting. A fruit cage offers total protection, but does not harmonize with a cottage garden.

3

THE PLANT DIRECTORY

Plants for cottage gardens usually have an informal habit which allows them to tumble into one another to create a mix of colours, scents and textures. Such plants range from short-lived annuals to herbaceous perennials, bulbs, herbs and roses. Trees, shrubs and climbers can provide a permanent framework for the more ephemeral plants. Many cottage gardens also include some fruit and vegetables, as well as ornamental hedges separating different areas of the garden.

LEFT *There are few sights to beat the traditional cottage-garden border in its full high-summer glory.*

HOW TO USE THIS DIRECTORY

*T*he Plant Directory lists all the plants that are featured in this book, together with a selection of other plants that are suitable for use in a cottage garden. It is not intended to be exhaustive, and experienced gardeners will have their own favourites. However, this listing has been made with the specific requirements of a cottage garden in mind; it will guide the beginner to a range of attractive and readily available plants, shrubs and trees with which to create a beautiful garden. Complete information on planting and maintaining the plants is given for each entry.

The Plant Directory is divided into different categories that group similar plants together. The categories are: annuals and biennials (*pages 62–7*), herbaceous perennials (*pages 68–77*), bulbs, corms and tubers (*pages 78–9*), ferns (*page 80*), grasses (*page 81*), shrubs (*pages 82–9*), trees (*pages 90–1*), shrub and species roses (*pages 92–3*), climbing and rambling roses (*pages 94–5*), climbers (*pages 96–7*), herbs (*pages 98–9*), vegetables (*pages 100–3*), fruit (*pages 104–5*) and hedging plants (*pages 106–7*). The hedges category is

important for cottage gardens, and it includes a range of plant types, for example, herbs, roses and shrubs; if you cannot find a plant in one of the earlier sections, try looking in hedging plants.

The panel next to each entry gives essential information on growing conditions (*see opposite for a key to the symbols*). Each photograph is accompanied by a description of the plant, indicating when flowering types are in bloom and explaining what type of soil each plant prefers.

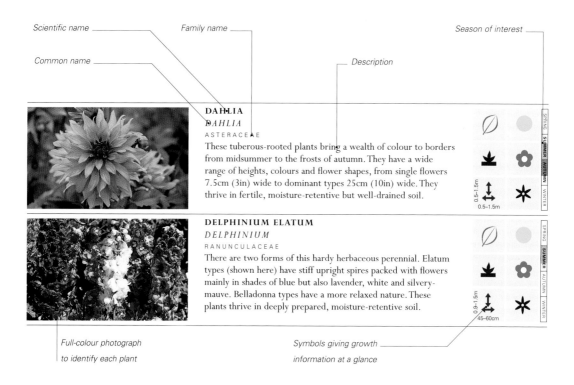

Scientific name _____

Common name _____

Family name _____

Description _____

Season of interest _____

DAHLIA
DAHLIA
ASTERACEAE
These tuberous-rooted plants bring a wealth of colour to borders from midsummer to the frosts of autumn. They have a wide range of heights, colours and flower shapes, from single flowers 7.5cm (3in) wide to dominant types 25cm (10in) wide. They thrive in fertile, moisture-retentive but well-drained soil.

0.5–1.5m / 0.5–1.5m

SPRING SUMMER AUTUMN WINTER

DELPHINIUM ELATUM
DELPHINIUM
RANUNCULACEAE
There are two forms of this hardy herbaceous perennial. Elatum types (shown here) have stiff upright spires packed with flowers mainly in shades of blue but also lavender, white and silvery-mauve. Belladonna types have a more relaxed nature. These plants thrive in deeply prepared, moisture-retentive soil.

0.9–1.5m / 45–60cm

SPRING SUMMER AUTUMN WINTER

Full-colour photograph to identify each plant

Symbols giving growth information at a glance

KEY TO THE SYMBOLS

 EASY TO GROW

These are tolerant plants that require no special care or conditions in order to flourish.

 MODERATE TO GROW

These are plants that require some special care, such as protection from frost.

DIFFICULT TO GROW

These are plants that require a great deal of specialized care, and offer a challenge for the more experienced gardener.

 EVERGREEN

SEMI-EVERGREEN

DECIDUOUS

Deciduous plants lose their leaves in autumn (sometimes in summer) while evergreen plants keep their foliage all the year round. Plants described as semi-evergreen may keep some or all of their foliage through the winter in sheltered gardens or if the weather is mild. No leaf symbol is given for annuals, nor for biennials (although some biennials do keep their leaves over the first winter) .

FEATURE LEAVES

FEATURE SCENT

FEATURE FLOWER

FEATURE FRUIT OR EDIBLE PRODUCE

These symbols indicate the main feature of interest for each plant in the directory. This will help you to choose plants that have complementary features, or plants that will perform a specific function in your garden. The symbols show the main feature or features of interest, but these are not necessarily the plant's only assets.

 RAPID GROWTH

MODERATE GROWTH

SLOW GROWTH

Speed of growth, like ease of growth, is a highly subjective category, and will vary according to local conditions. Rapid growth indicates plants that reach their full extent in a single season (annuals for instance), or plants that make substantial progress towards filling the space allowed for them in a single season. Slow growth indicates plants, such as trees and some shrubs, that take several seasons to reach their ultimate size. Moderate growth refers therefore to rates of progress between these two extremes.

The period of the year when a plant is likely to be at its most attractive is also indicated. This will allow you, for instance, to create a planting scheme that will have something of interest for each season of the year.

HEIGHT AND SPREAD

The size of plants will vary according to the growing conditions in your garden, so these measurements are a rough guide only. The measurements refer to the size of plants and trees when mature, although again there are specific cases where the ultimate size is never reached. For instance, climbing roses can be pruned to fit smaller spaces. The heights and spreads given for foliage and flowering climbers are indications only, as they depend on the size and shape of the supporting framework.

FULL SUN

PARTIAL SUN

SHADE

An indication of light preference is given to show each plant's optimum growing situation. Two symbols may be shown together to indicate the full range of tolerance, as some plants that prefer sun may also be reasonably tolerant of shade.

ANNUALS AND BIENNIALS

ALCEA ROSEA
HOLLYHOCK
MALVACEAE

Earlier known as *Althaea rosea*, this hardy perennial is usually grown as a hardy biennial and even occasionally as an annual. It develops spikes of 10cm (4in) wide pink, yellow, scarlet, dark maroon, red or white flowers from midsummer to early autumn. It grows well in fertile, heavy and moisture-retentive soil.

1.5–2.4m
50–60cm

AMARANTHUS CAUDATUS 'VIRIDIS'
LOVE-LIES-BLEEDING
AMARANTHACEAE

This hardy annual is usually raised as a half-hardy annual. It bears pale green flowers in long pendulous tassel-like clusters from midsummer to autumn. The flowers are borne amid light green oval leaves and are often used in flower arrangements. The plant requires fertile, well-drained but moisture-retentive soil.

0.9–1.2m
38–45cm

ANTIRRHINUM MAJUS
SNAPDRAGON
SCROPHULARIACEAE

This short-lived perennial is usually grown as a half-hardy annual; it can also can be raised as a hardy annual. There is a range of heights and types, all with the characteristic dragon-like flowers, in a wide spectrum of colours. It requires fertile, well-drained but moisture-retentive, light to medium soil.

0.3–1m
23–45cm

ASPERULA ORIENTALIS
ANNUAL WOODRUFF
RUBIACEAE

Also known as *Asperula azurea* and *Asperula setosa*, this distinctive hardy annual has narrow, hairy, mid-green leaves that arise in clusters around a stem. The tubular fragrant pale blue flowers are borne in terminal clusters during midsummer. It requires light, moisture-retentive but well-drained soil.

30cm
10–15cm

BELLIS PERENNIS
COMMON DAISY
ASTERACEAE

A hardy perennial, invariably grown as a biennial, that has white daisy-like flowers throughout summer. There are several varieties, some double-flowered, in colours including white, carmine, pink, salmon and rich cherry. It is ideal as an edging to borders. Plant it in well-drained but moisture-retentive soil.

2.5–10cm
7.5–10cm

CALENDULA OFFICINALIS
MARIGOLD
ASTERACEAE

A popular hardy annual with light green leaves and masses of daisy-like orange or bright yellow flowers about 7.5cm (3in) wide throughout summer. There is a range of varieties, some double-flowered, others dwarf. It often grows from self-sown seeds; sow them in light, well-drained, moisture-retentive soil.

45–60cm
25–30cm

SPRING SUMMER AUTUMN WINTER

leaf type — light preference — speed of growth — ease of growth

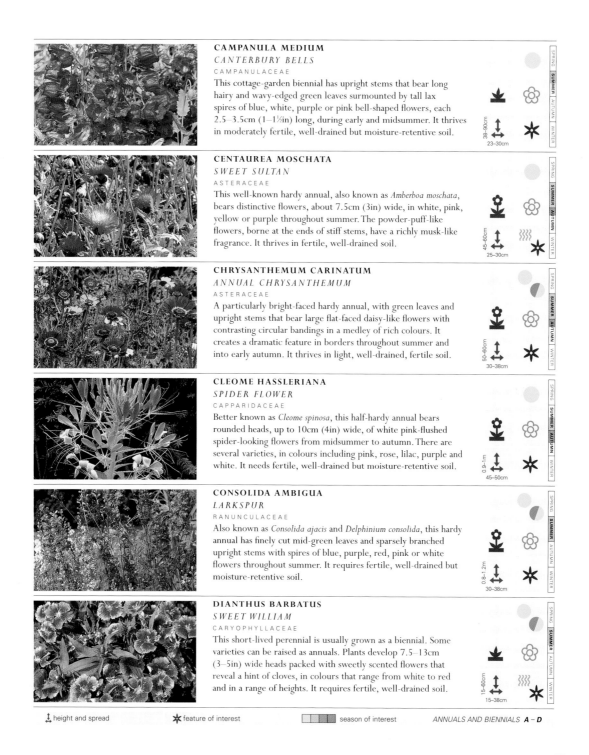

CAMPANULA MEDIUM
CANTERBURY BELLS
CAMPANULACEAE

This cottage-garden biennial has upright stems that bear long hairy and wavy-edged green leaves surmounted by tall lax spires of blue, white, purple or pink bell-shaped flowers, each 2.5–3.5cm (1–1⅓in) long, during early and midsummer. It thrives in moderately fertile, well-drained but moisture-retentive soil.

38–90cm
23–30cm

CENTAUREA MOSCHATA
SWEET SULTAN
ASTERACEAE

This well-known hardy annual, also known as *Amberboa moschata*, bears distinctive flowers, about 7.5cm (3in) wide, in white, pink, yellow or purple throughout summer. The powder-puff-like flowers, borne at the ends of stiff stems, have a richly musk-like fragrance. It thrives in fertile, well-drained soil.

45–60cm
25–30cm

CHRYSANTHEMUM CARINATUM
ANNUAL CHRYSANTHEMUM
ASTERACEAE

A particularly bright-faced hardy annual, with green leaves and upright stems that bear large flat-faced daisy-like flowers with contrasting circular bandings in a medley of rich colours. It creates a dramatic feature in borders throughout summer and into early autumn. It thrives in light, well-drained, fertile soil.

50–60cm
30–38cm

CLEOME HASSLERIANA
SPIDER FLOWER
CAPPARIDACEAE

Better known as *Cleome spinosa*, this half-hardy annual bears rounded heads, up to 10cm (4in) wide, of white pink-flushed spider-looking flowers from midsummer to autumn. There are several varieties, in colours including pink, rose, lilac, purple and white. It needs fertile, well-drained but moisture-retentive soil.

0.9–1m
45–50cm

CONSOLIDA AMBIGUA
LARKSPUR
RANUNCULACEAE

Also known as *Consolida ajacis* and *Delphinium consolida*, this hardy annual has finely cut mid-green leaves and sparsely branched upright stems with spires of blue, purple, red, pink or white flowers throughout summer. It requires fertile, well-drained but moisture-retentive soil.

0.8–1.2m
30–38cm

DIANTHUS BARBATUS
SWEET WILLIAM
CARYOPHYLLACEAE

This short-lived perennial is usually grown as a biennial. Some varieties can be raised as annuals. Plants develop 7.5–13cm (3–5in) wide heads packed with sweetly scented flowers that reveal a hint of cloves, in colours that range from white to red and in a range of heights. It requires fertile, well-drained soil.

15–60cm
15–38cm

SPRING SUMMER AUTUMN WINTER

↕ height and spread   ✳ feature of interest   ▢▢▢▢ season of interest   *ANNUALS AND BIENNIALS* **A – D**

ANNUALS AND BIENNIALS

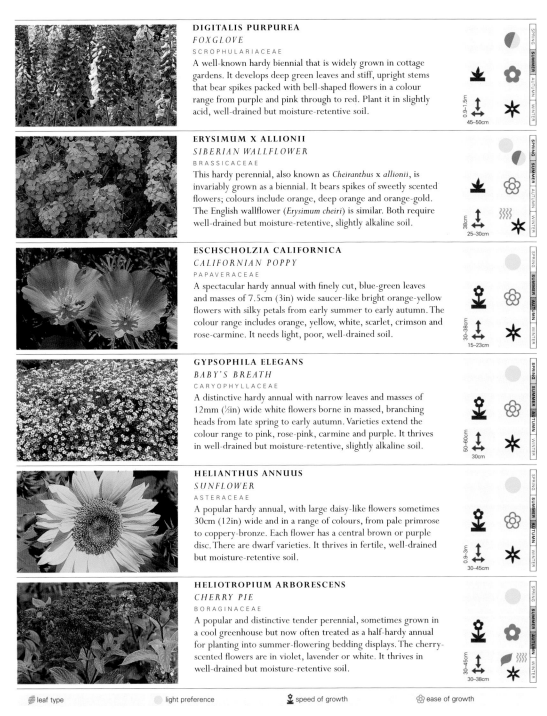

DIGITALIS PURPUREA
FOXGLOVE
SCROPHULARIACEAE

A well-known hardy biennial that is widely grown in cottage gardens. It develops deep green leaves and stiff, upright stems that bear spikes packed with bell-shaped flowers in a colour range from purple and pink through to red. Plant it in slightly acid, well-drained but moisture-retentive soil.

0.9–1.5m
45–50cm

SPRING | SUMMER | AUTUMN | WINTER

ERYSIMUM X ALLIONII
SIBERIAN WALLFLOWER
BRASSICACEAE

This hardy perennial, also known as *Cheiranthus* x *allionii*, is invariably grown as a biennial. It bears spikes of sweetly scented flowers; colours include orange, deep orange and orange-gold. The English wallflower (*Erysimum cheiri*) is similar. Both require well-drained but moisture-retentive, slightly alkaline soil.

38cm
25–30cm

SPRING | SUMMER | AUTUMN | WINTER

ESCHSCHOLZIA CALIFORNICA
CALIFORNIAN POPPY
PAPAVERACEAE

A spectacular hardy annual with finely cut, blue-green leaves and masses of 7.5cm (3in) wide saucer-like bright orange-yellow flowers with silky petals from early summer to early autumn. The colour range includes orange, yellow, white, scarlet, crimson and rose-carmine. It needs light, poor, well-drained soil.

30–38cm
15–23cm

SPRING | SUMMER | AUTUMN | WINTER

GYPSOPHILA ELEGANS
BABY'S BREATH
CARYOPHYLLACEAE

A distinctive hardy annual with narrow leaves and masses of 12mm (½in) wide white flowers borne in massed, branching heads from late spring to early autumn. Varieties extend the colour range to pink, rose-pink, carmine and purple. It thrives in well-drained but moisture-retentive, slightly alkaline soil.

50–60cm
30cm

SPRING | SUMMER | AUTUMN | WINTER

HELIANTHUS ANNUUS
SUNFLOWER
ASTERACEAE

A popular hardy annual, with large daisy-like flowers sometimes 30cm (12in) wide and in a range of colours, from pale primrose to coppery-bronze. Each flower has a central brown or purple disc. There are dwarf varieties. It thrives in fertile, well-drained but moisture-retentive soil.

0.9–3m
30–45cm

SPRING | SUMMER | AUTUMN | WINTER

HELIOTROPIUM ARBORESCENS
CHERRY PIE
BORAGINACEAE

A popular and distinctive tender perennial, sometimes grown in a cool greenhouse but now often treated as a half-hardy annual for planting into summer-flowering bedding displays. The cherry-scented flowers are in violet, lavender or white. It thrives in well-drained but moisture-retentive soil.

30–45cm
30–38cm

SPRING | SUMMER | AUTUMN | WINTER

leaf type   light preference   speed of growth   ease of growth

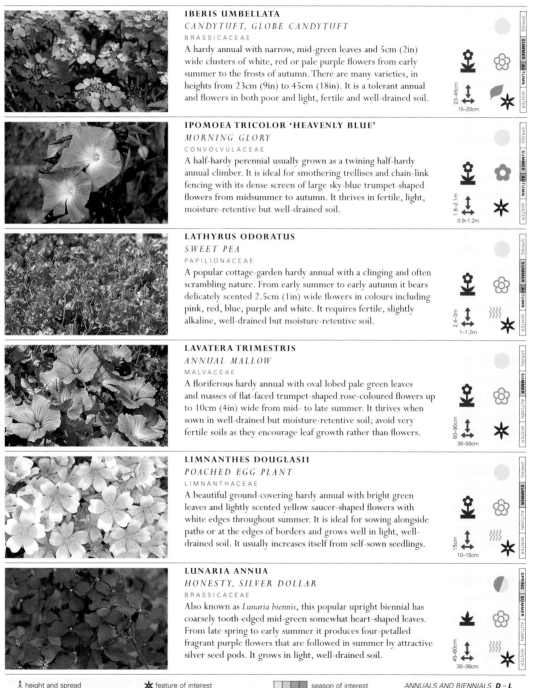

IBERIS UMBELLATA
CANDYTUFT, GLOBE CANDYTUFT

BRASSICACEAE

A hardy annual with narrow, mid-green leaves and 5cm (2in) wide clusters of white, red or pale purple flowers from early summer to the frosts of autumn. There are many varieties, in heights from 23cm (9in) to 45cm (18in). It is a tolerant annual and flowers in both poor and light, fertile and well-drained soil.

23–45cm
15–20cm

IPOMOEA TRICOLOR 'HEAVENLY BLUE'
MORNING GLORY

CONVOLVULACEAE

A half-hardy perennial usually grown as a twining half-hardy annual climber. It is ideal for smothering trellises and chain-link fencing with its dense screen of large sky-blue trumpet-shaped flowers from midsummer to autumn. It thrives in fertile, light, moisture-retentive but well-drained soil.

1.8–2.1m
0.9–1.2m

LATHYRUS ODORATUS
SWEET PEA

PAPILIONACEAE

A popular cottage-garden hardy annual with a clinging and often scrambling nature. From early summer to early autumn it bears delicately scented 2.5cm (1in) wide flowers in colours including pink, red, blue, purple and white. It requires fertile, slightly alkaline, well-drained but moisture-retentive soil.

2.4–3m
1–1.2m

LAVATERA TRIMESTRIS
ANNUAL MALLOW

MALVACEAE

A floriferous hardy annual with oval lobed pale green leaves and masses of flat-faced trumpet-shaped rose-coloured flowers up to 10cm (4in) wide from mid- to late summer. It thrives when sown in well-drained but moisture-retentive soil; avoid very fertile soils as they encourage leaf growth rather than flowers.

60–90cm
38–50cm

LIMNANTHES DOUGLASII
POACHED EGG PLANT

LIMNANTHACEAE

A beautiful ground-covering hardy annual with bright green leaves and lightly scented yellow saucer-shaped flowers with white edges throughout summer. It is ideal for sowing alongside paths or at the edges of borders and grows well in light, well-drained soil. It usually increases itself from self-sown seedlings.

15cm
10–15cm

LUNARIA ANNUA
HONESTY, SILVER DOLLAR

BRASSICACEAE

Also known as *Lunaria biennis*, this popular upright biennial has coarsely tooth-edged mid-green somewhat heart-shaped leaves. From late spring to early summer it produces four-petalled fragrant purple flowers that are followed in summer by attractive silver seed pods. It grows in light, well-drained soil.

45–60cm
30–38cm

⬍ height and spread   ✳ feature of interest   ▭▭▭ season of interest   *ANNUALS AND BIENNIALS* **D – L**

ANNUALS AND BIENNIALS

MALCOLMIA MARITIMA
VIRGINIAN STOCK
BRASSICACEAE

A sweetly scented and showy hardy annual with white cross-shaped flowers that appear among grey-green leaves. It grows rapidly and flowers four weeks after sowing and then continues for six to eight weeks. Repeated sowings are needed to produce a succession of flowers. It prefers light, well-drained soil.

20–30cm
15–20cm

MATTHIOLA LONGIPETALA SUBSP. BICORNIS
NIGHT-SCENTED STOCK
BRASSICACEAE

A popular hardy annual, better known as *Matthiola bicornis*, with grey-green leaves and four-petalled purple-lilac flowers that exude a sweet and heavy fragrance, especially during evenings and at night. It is ideal for sowing as a companion to Virginian stock (*Malcolmia maritima*). It thrives in light, well-drained soil.

38cm
20–23cm

MYOSOTIS ALPESTRIS
FORGET-ME-NOT
BORAGINACEAE

A popular hardy biennial or short-lived perennial that swamps borders with misty-blue flowers in lax sprays during late spring and early summer. There are several varieties, in colours including bright blue, indigo-blue, pink and white. It prefers fertile, moisture-retentive but well-drained soil.

20–30cm
15–20cm

NICOTIANA ALATA
FLOWERING TOBACCO PLANT
SOLANACEAE

A popular half-hardy annual, also known as *Nicotiana affinis*, with clusters of tubular 7.5cm (3in) long sweetly scented flowers in a wide range of varieties and colours including white, cream, pink, crimson, yellow and yellowish-green. It requires fertile, well-drained but moisture-retentive soil.

45–75cm
30–38cm

NIGELLA DAMASCENA
LOVE-IN-A-MIST
RANUNCULACEAE

A beautiful cottage-garden hardy annual with bright green fern-like leaves and cornflower-like 3.5cm (1⅜in) wide flowers from early to late summer. There are several superb varieties, in mixed colours as well as bright blue, mauve, purple, rose-pink and white. Some are semi-double. It prefers light, well-drained soil.

45–60cm
15–20cm

OENOTHERA BIENNIS
EVENING PRIMROSE
ONAGRACEAE

A hardy biennial, but sometimes grown as an annual, with pale primrose-yellow flowers borne in clusters on upright stems from early summer to mid-autumn. The 4–5cm (1½–2in) wide flowers have a sweet redolence, especially during evenings. It often grows from self-sown seedlings and thrives in light, well-drained soil.

60–90cm
30–38cm

SPRING SUMMER AUTUMN WINTER

leaf type   light preference   speed of growth   ease of growth

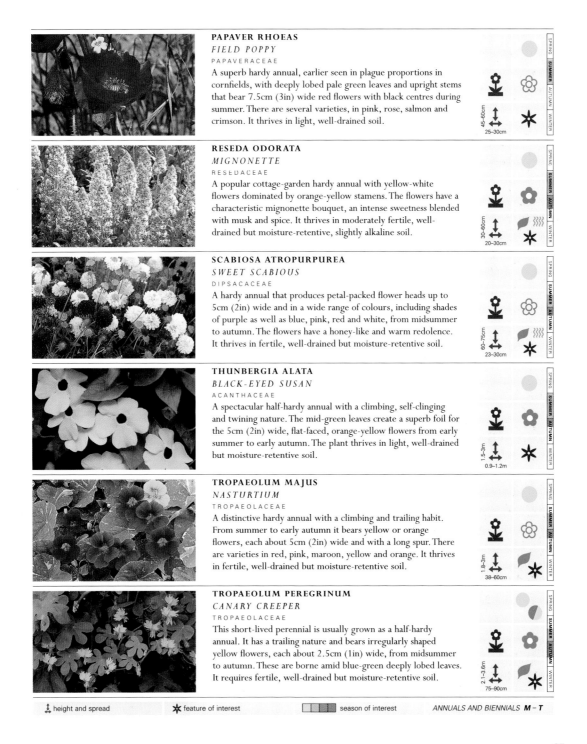

PAPAVER RHOEAS
FIELD POPPY
PAPAVERACEAE

A superb hardy annual, earlier seen in plague proportions in cornfields, with deeply lobed pale green leaves and upright stems that bear 7.5cm (3in) wide red flowers with black centres during summer. There are several varieties, in pink, rose, salmon and crimson. It thrives in light, well-drained soil.

45–60cm
25–30cm

RESEDA ODORATA
MIGNONETTE
RESEDACEAE

A popular cottage-garden hardy annual with yellow-white flowers dominated by orange-yellow stamens. The flowers have a characteristic mignonette bouquet, an intense sweetness blended with musk and spice. It thrives in moderately fertile, well-drained but moisture-retentive, slightly alkaline soil.

30–60cm
20–30cm

SCABIOSA ATROPURPUREA
SWEET SCABIOUS
DIPSACACEAE

A hardy annual that produces petal-packed flower heads up to 5cm (2in) wide and in a wide range of colours, including shades of purple as well as blue, pink, red and white, from midsummer to autumn. The flowers have a honey-like and warm redolence. It thrives in fertile, well-drained but moisture-retentive soil.

60–75cm
23–30cm

THUNBERGIA ALATA
BLACK-EYED SUSAN
ACANTHACEAE

A spectacular half-hardy annual with a climbing, self-clinging and twining nature. The mid-green leaves create a superb foil for the 5cm (2in) wide, flat-faced, orange-yellow flowers from early summer to early autumn. The plant thrives in light, well-drained but moisture-retentive soil.

1.5–3m
0.9–1.2m

TROPAEOLUM MAJUS
NASTURTIUM
TROPAEOLACEAE

A distinctive hardy annual with a climbing and trailing habit. From summer to early autumn it bears yellow or orange flowers, each about 5cm (2in) wide and with a long spur. There are varieties in red, pink, maroon, yellow and orange. It thrives in fertile, well-drained but moisture-retentive soil.

1.8–3m
38–60cm

TROPAEOLUM PEREGRINUM
CANARY CREEPER
TROPAEOLACEAE

This short-lived perennial is usually grown as a half-hardy annual. It has a trailing nature and bears irregularly shaped yellow flowers, each about 2.5cm (1in) wide, from midsummer to autumn. These are borne amid blue-green deeply lobed leaves. It requires fertile, well-drained but moisture-retentive soil.

2.1–3.6m
75–90cm

SPRING SUMMER AUTUMN WINTER

↕ height and spread   ✳ feature of interest   ▭▭▭ season of interest   *ANNUALS AND BIENNIALS* **M – T**

67

HERBACEOUS PERENNIALS

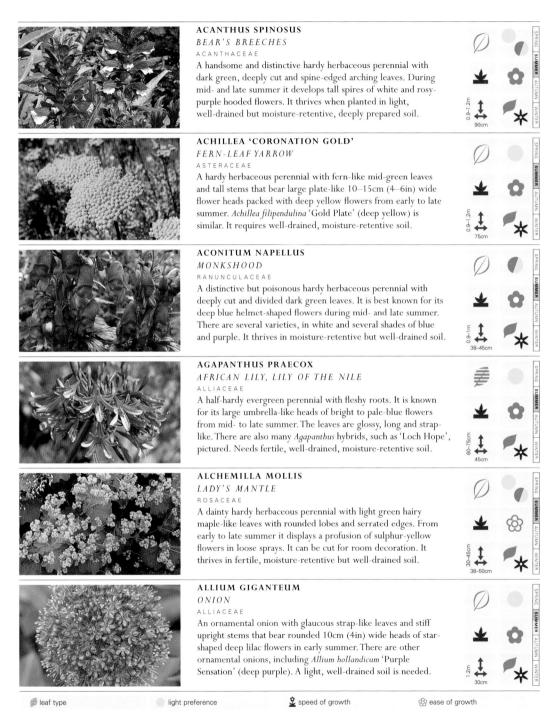

ACANTHUS SPINOSUS
BEAR'S BREECHES
ACANTHACEAE

A handsome and distinctive hardy herbaceous perennial with dark green, deeply cut and spine-edged arching leaves. During mid- and late summer it develops tall spires of white and rosy-purple hooded flowers. It thrives when planted in light, well-drained but moisture-retentive, deeply prepared soil.

0.9–1.2m
90cm

SPRING SUMMER AUTUMN WINTER

ACHILLEA 'CORONATION GOLD'
FERN-LEAF YARROW
ASTERACEAE

A hardy herbaceous perennial with fern-like mid-green leaves and tall stems that bear large plate-like 10–15cm (4–6in) wide flower heads packed with deep yellow flowers from early to late summer. *Achillea filipendulina* 'Gold Plate' (deep yellow) is similar. It requires well-drained, moisture-retentive soil.

0.9–1.2m
75cm

SPRING SUMMER AUTUMN WINTER

ACONITUM NAPELLUS
MONKSHOOD
RANUNCULACEAE

A distinctive but poisonous hardy herbaceous perennial with deeply cut and divided dark green leaves. It is best known for its deep blue helmet-shaped flowers during mid- and late summer. There are several varieties, in white and several shades of blue and purple. It thrives in moisture-retentive but well-drained soil.

0.9–1m
38–45cm

SPRING SUMMER AUTUMN WINTER

AGAPANTHUS PRAECOX
AFRICAN LILY, LILY OF THE NILE
ALLIACEAE

A half-hardy evergreen perennial with fleshy roots. It is known for its large umbrella-like heads of bright to pale-blue flowers from mid- to late summer. The leaves are glossy, long and strap-like. There are also many *Agapanthus* hybrids, such as 'Loch Hope', pictured. Needs fertile, well-drained, moisture-retentive soil.

60–75cm
45cm

SPRING SUMMER AUTUMN WINTER

ALCHEMILLA MOLLIS
LADY'S MANTLE
ROSACEAE

A dainty hardy herbaceous perennial with light green hairy maple-like leaves with rounded lobes and serrated edges. From early to late summer it displays a profusion of sulphur-yellow flowers in loose sprays. It can be cut for room decoration. It thrives in fertile, moisture-retentive but well-drained soil.

30–45cm
38–50cm

SPRING SUMMER AUTUMN WINTER

ALLIUM GIGANTEUM
ONION
ALLIACEAE

An ornamental onion with glaucous strap-like leaves and stiff upright stems that bear rounded 10cm (4in) wide heads of star-shaped deep lilac flowers in early summer. There are other ornamental onions, including *Allium hollandicum* 'Purple Sensation' (deep purple). A light, well-drained soil is needed.

1.2m
30cm

SPRING SUMMER AUTUMN WINTER

≣ leaf type   ● light preference   ⚑ speed of growth   ⚙ ease of growth

ALLIUM MOLY
GOLDEN GARLIC, YELLOW ONION
ALLIACEAE
A hardy bulbous perennial with mid-green strap-shaped
leaves. Demurely sweet bright yellow star-like flowers appear
in umbrella-like clusters up to 5cm (2in) wide during early
and midsummer. Eventually it spreads to form a large clump; it
thrives in light, fertile, well-drained but moisture-retentive soil.

30cm / 15–20cm

ANAPHALIS TRIPLINERVIS
LIFE EVERLASTING
ASTERACEAE
An attractive hardy herbaceous perennial with silver-green leaves
covered with white woolly hairs. Additionally, in late summer it
bears bunched heads, about 7.5cm (3in) wide, of white flowers.
The variety 'Sommerschnee', also known as 'Summer Snow', is
especially attractive. It thrives in light, well-drained soil.

30cm / 30–38cm

ANEMONE X HYBRIDA
JAPANESE ANEMONE
RANUNCULACEAE
A distinctive late summer to mid-autumn flowering herbaceous
perennial with upright stems that bear bright-faced white to deep
rose-coloured flowers, each up to 7.5cm (3in) wide. Varieties
include 'Honorine Jobert' (semi-double and white). Fertile,
moisture-retentive but well-drained soil is needed.

0.6–1.2m / 38–45cm

ANTHEMIS PUNCTATA SUBSP. CUPANIANA
GOLDEN MARGUERITE
ASTERACEAE
A hardy short-lived herbaceous perennial with daisy-like bright-
faced white flowers, 5–7.5cm (2–2½in) wide, with bright yellow
centres throughout much of summer. The flowers appear above
aromatic, finely dissected, grey leaves. It requires well-drained
but moisture-retentive soil. Is successful grown in containers.

20–30cm / 30–38cm

AQUILEGIA VULGARIS
COLUMBINE, GRANNY'S BONNET
RANUNCULACEAE
A hardy herbaceous perennial with funnel-shaped spurred
flowers that exude a soft clove-like fragrance. There is a wide
range of colours: blue, pink, white, yellow and crimson. The
leaves are grey-green and formed of several leaflets. It requires
well-drained but moisture-retentive soil and is mildly poisonous.

45–60cm / 30–45cm

ASTER SEDIFOLIUS
PERENNIAL ASTER
ASTERACEAE
Also known as *Aster acris*, this hardy herbaceous perennial
creates a mass of clear lavender-blue star-like flowers with golden
centres on bushy plants during late summer and into autumn.
The variety 'Nanus' is shorter, at 30cm (12in) high. It thrives
in fertile, moisture-retentive but well-drained soil.

60–75cm / 38–45cm

SPRING SUMMER AUTUMN WINTER

⬍ height and spread   ✳ feature of interest   ▭▭▭▭ season of interest   *HERBACEOUS PERENNIALS* **A**

HERBACEOUS PERENNIALS

ASTILBE X ARENDSII
HERBACEOUS SPIRAEA
SAXIFRAGACEAE
A distinctive hardy herbaceous perennial with mid- to deep green deeply divided and fern-like foliage. Around midsummer it reveals plume-like pyramidal and rather fluffy heads of flowers. There are several superb varieties, in white, through pink, to red. It requires fertile, moisture-retentive soil.

60–75cm
38–50cm

BERGENIA CORDIFOLIA
ELEPHANT'S EARS
SAXIFRAGACEAE
A distinctive evergreen border plant with large rounded dark green leaves and drooping heads of pale pink bell-shaped flowers during mid- and late spring. 'Purpurea' has pinkish-purple flowers. *Bergenia* hybrids include 'Silberlicht' (silver-white) and 'Baby Doll' (pale pink). Well-drained soil suits bergenias.

30cm
30–38cm

CAMPANULA LACTIFLORA
BELLFLOWER
CAMPANULACEAE
A hardy herbaceous perennial that produces masses of light lavender-blue flowers during early and midsummer. There are several varieties, such as 'Loddon Anna' (soft pink and up to 1.2m (4ft) high) and 'White Pouffe' (white and 60cm (2ft) high). It requires fertile, well-drained but moisture-retentive soil.

0.9–1.5m
38–45cm

CHAMAEMELUM NOBILE
COMMON CHAMOMILE
ASTERACEAE
Also known as *Anthemis nobilis*, this hardy mat-forming herbaceous perennial has finely dissected aromatic leaves. It has daisy-like flowers from late spring to mid-autumn. It is often used to form a chamomile lawn. 'Treneague' is non-flowering and reveals a banana-like redolence. Plant in well-drained soil.

15cm
30–38cm

CONVALLARIA MAJALIS
LILY-OF-THE-VALLEY
CONVALLARIACEAE
A hardy clump-forming rhizomatous-rooted border perennial, well known for its upright elongated spoon-shaped and pointed green leaves. Its penetratingly sweet, waxy, nodding, bell-shaped flowers are borne on arching stems during spring. It thrives in well-drained but moisture-retentive soil. It is poisonous.

15cm
30–38cm

COREOPSIS VERTICILLATA
TICKSEED
ASTERACEAE
A long-lived herbaceous perennial with fern-like finely divided bright green leaves and masses of clear yellow, star-like flowers from early to late summer. There are several varieties, including 'Grandiflora' (bright yellow) and 'Zagreb' (strongly yellow). It thrives in well-drained but moisture-retentive soil.

45–60cm
30–45cm

---

leaf type   light preference   speed of growth   ease of growth

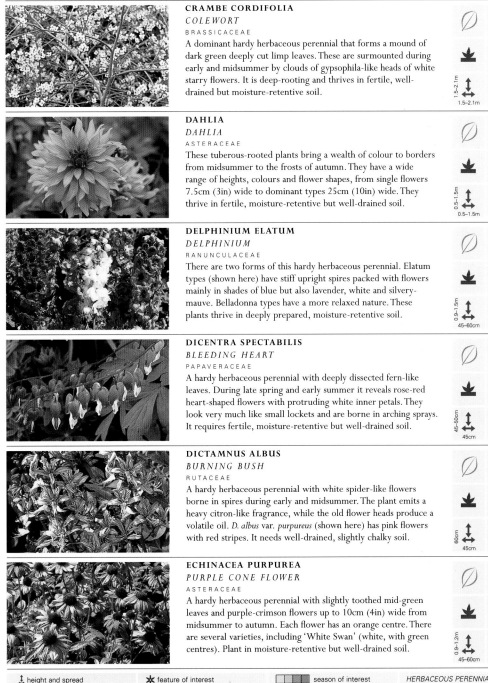

CRAMBE CORDIFOLIA
COLEWORT
BRASSICACEAE

A dominant hardy herbaceous perennial that forms a mound of dark green deeply cut limp leaves. These are surmounted during early and midsummer by clouds of gypsophila-like heads of white starry flowers. It is deep-rooting and thrives in fertile, well-drained but moisture-retentive soil.

1.5–2.1m / 1.5–2.1m

DAHLIA
DAHLIA
ASTERACEAE

These tuberous-rooted plants bring a wealth of colour to borders from midsummer to the frosts of autumn. They have a wide range of heights, colours and flower shapes, from single flowers 7.5cm (3in) wide to dominant types 25cm (10in) wide. They thrive in fertile, moisture-retentive but well-drained soil.

0.5–1.5m / 0.5–1.5m

DELPHINIUM ELATUM
DELPHINIUM
RANUNCULACEAE

There are two forms of this hardy herbaceous perennial. Elatum types (shown here) have stiff upright spires packed with flowers mainly in shades of blue but also lavender, white and silvery-mauve. Belladonna types have a more relaxed nature. These plants thrive in deeply prepared, moisture-retentive soil.

0.9–1.5m / 45–60cm

DICENTRA SPECTABILIS
BLEEDING HEART
PAPAVERACEAE

A hardy herbaceous perennial with deeply dissected fern-like leaves. During late spring and early summer it reveals rose-red heart-shaped flowers with protruding white inner petals. They look very much like small lockets and are borne in arching sprays. It requires fertile, moisture-retentive but well-drained soil.

45–50cm / 45cm

DICTAMNUS ALBUS
BURNING BUSH
RUTACEAE

A hardy herbaceous perennial with white spider-like flowers borne in spires during early and midsummer. The plant emits a heavy citron-like fragrance, while the old flower heads produce a volatile oil. *D. albus* var. *purpureus* (shown here) has pink flowers with red stripes. It needs well-drained, slightly chalky soil.

60cm / 45cm

ECHINACEA PURPUREA
PURPLE CONE FLOWER
ASTERACEAE

A hardy herbaceous perennial with slightly toothed mid-green leaves and purple-crimson flowers up to 10cm (4in) wide from midsummer to autumn. Each flower has an orange centre. There are several varieties, including 'White Swan' (white, with green centres). Plant in moisture-retentive but well-drained soil.

0.9–1.2m / 45–60cm

⬍ height and spread   ✳ feature of interest   ▭ season of interest   *HERBACEOUS PERENNIALS A – E*

HERBACEOUS PERENNIALS

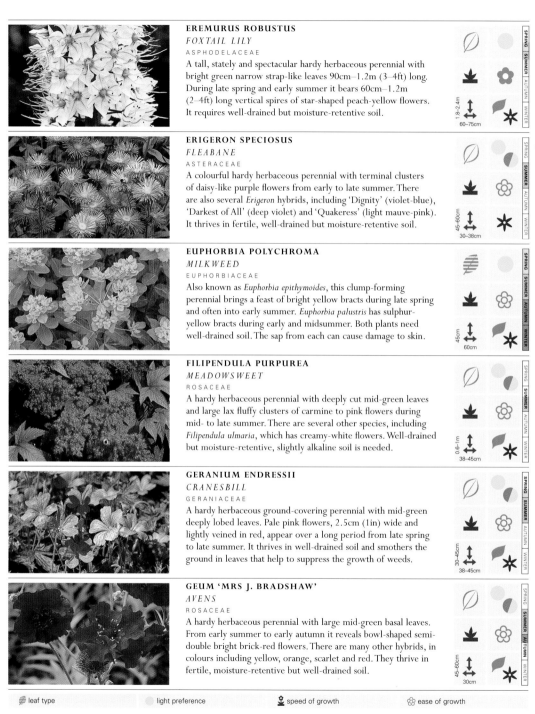

EREMURUS ROBUSTUS
FOXTAIL LILY
ASPHODELACEAE
A tall, stately and spectacular hardy herbaceous perennial with bright green narrow strap-like leaves 90cm–1.2m (3–4ft) long. During late spring and early summer it bears 60cm–1.2m (2–4ft) long vertical spires of star-shaped peach-yellow flowers. It requires well-drained but moisture-retentive soil.

1.8–2.4m
60–75cm

SPRING SUMMER AUTUMN WINTER

ERIGERON SPECIOSUS
FLEABANE
ASTERACEAE
A colourful hardy herbaceous perennial with terminal clusters of daisy-like purple flowers from early to late summer. There are also several *Erigeron* hybrids, including 'Dignity' (violet-blue), 'Darkest of All' (deep violet) and 'Quakeress' (light mauve-pink). It thrives in fertile, well-drained but moisture-retentive soil.

45–60cm
30–38cm

SPRING SUMMER AUTUMN WINTER

EUPHORBIA POLYCHROMA
MILKWEED
EUPHORBIACEAE
Also known as *Euphorbia epithymoides*, this clump-forming perennial brings a feast of bright yellow bracts during late spring and often into early summer. *Euphorbia palustris* has sulphur-yellow bracts during early and midsummer. Both plants need well-drained soil. The sap from each can cause damage to skin.

45cm
60cm

SPRING SUMMER AUTUMN WINTER

FILIPENDULA PURPUREA
MEADOWSWEET
ROSACEAE
A hardy herbaceous perennial with deeply cut mid-green leaves and large lax fluffy clusters of carmine to pink flowers during mid- to late summer. There are several other species, including *Filipendula ulmaria*, which has creamy-white flowers. Well-drained but moisture-retentive, slightly alkaline soil is needed.

0.6–1m
38–45cm

SPRING SUMMER AUTUMN WINTER

GERANIUM ENDRESSII
CRANESBILL
GERANIACEAE
A hardy herbaceous ground-covering perennial with mid-green deeply lobed leaves. Pale pink flowers, 2.5cm (1in) wide and lightly veined in red, appear over a long period from late spring to late summer. It thrives in well-drained soil and smothers the ground in leaves that help to suppress the growth of weeds.

30–45cm
38–45cm

SPRING SUMMER AUTUMN WINTER

GEUM 'MRS J. BRADSHAW'
AVENS
ROSACEAE
A hardy herbaceous perennial with large mid-green basal leaves. From early summer to early autumn it reveals bowl-shaped semi-double bright brick-red flowers. There are many other hybrids, in colours including yellow, orange, scarlet and red. They thrive in fertile, moisture-retentive but well-drained soil.

45–60cm
30cm

SPRING SUMMER AUTUMN WINTER

🟰 leaf type   ⬤ light preference   ⬇ speed of growth   ✿ ease of growth

GYPSOPHILA PANICULATA 'COMPACTA PLENA'
BABY'S BREATH
CARYOPHYLLACEAE

A spectacular hardy herbaceous perennial with grass-like grey-green leaves and clouds of small double white flowers borne on stiff stems from early to late summer. There are several other cultivars, such as 'Bristol Fairy' (white and double-flowered). Plant it in cultivated, well-drained and slightly alkaline soil.

30–45cm
38–45cm

HELENIUM 'BUTTERPAT'
SNEEZEWORT
ASTERACEAE

A hardy herbaceous perennial that creates a mass of large daisy-like, rich yellow flowers, up to 3.5cm (1⅜in) wide, during late summer and early autumn. There are many other hybrids, in colours including rich orange, copper red, mahogany and bronze-red. Plant it in moisture-retentive but well-drained soil.

90cm
45–60cm

HELLEBORUS FOETIDUS
STINKING HELLEBORE
RANUNCULACEAE

A hardy evergreen border plant with deeply cut narrowly lance-shaped leaves. During spring it bears clusters of 2.5cm (1in) wide yellow-green flowers, sometimes edged in purple. There are several other hellebores, including *Helleborus niger* (white flowers). Plant in well-drained but moisture-retentive soil.

45–60cm
45–60cm

HEMEROCALLIS THUNBERGII
DAY LILY
HEMEROCALLIDACEAE

A bright-faced hardy herbaceous perennial with large trumpet-shaped sulphur-apricot flowers at the tops of tall stiff upright stems during summer. There are also many superb *Hemerocallis* hybrids, in colours from golden-yellow to pink, orange and red. They thrive in fertile, moisture-retentive but well-drained soil.

75–90cm
45–60cm

HESPERIS MATRONALIS
SWEET ROCKET
BRASSICACEAE

A hardy but short-lived perennial sometimes raised and grown as a biennial. It has an upright stance and bears dark green leaves and long spires of cross-shaped white, purple or mauve flowers during early summer. It is fragrant, especially during evenings, and requires light, moisture-retentive but well-drained soil.

60–90cm
38–45cm

HOSTA FORTUNEI VAR. ALBOPICTA
PLANTAIN LILY
HOSTACEAE

A hardy herbaceous perennial, mainly grown for its pale green pointed and somewhat spoon-shaped leaves with buff-yellow variegations. It bears lilac-coloured flowers during early and midsummer. It grows best in fertile, moisture-retentive but well-drained soil. Light shade is best for variegated plants.

45cm
45cm

⟱ height and spread   ✳ feature of interest   ▭▭▭ season of interest   *HERBACEOUS PERENNIALS* **E – H**

HERBACEOUS PERENNIALS

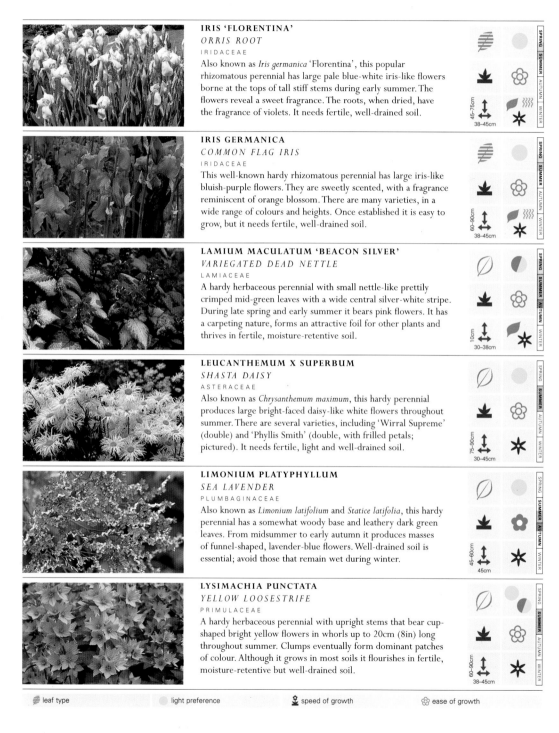

IRIS 'FLORENTINA'
ORRIS ROOT
IRIDACEAE

Also known as *Iris germanica* 'Florentina', this popular rhizomatous perennial has large pale blue-white iris-like flowers borne at the tops of tall stiff stems during early summer. The flowers reveal a sweet fragrance. The roots, when dried, have the fragrance of violets. It needs fertile, well-drained soil.

45–75cm
38–45cm

IRIS GERMANICA
COMMON FLAG IRIS
IRIDACEAE

This well-known hardy rhizomatous perennial has large iris-like bluish-purple flowers. They are sweetly scented, with a fragrance reminiscent of orange blossom. There are many varieties, in a wide range of colours and heights. Once established it is easy to grow, but it needs fertile, well-drained soil.

60–90cm
38–45cm

LAMIUM MACULATUM 'BEACON SILVER'
VARIEGATED DEAD NETTLE
LAMIACEAE

A hardy herbaceous perennial with small nettle-like prettily crimped mid-green leaves with a wide central silver-white stripe. During late spring and early summer it bears pink flowers. It has a carpeting nature, forms an attractive foil for other plants and thrives in fertile, moisture-retentive soil.

10cm
30–38cm

LEUCANTHEMUM X SUPERBUM
SHASTA DAISY
ASTERACEAE

Also known as *Chrysanthemum maximum*, this hardy perennial produces large bright-faced daisy-like white flowers throughout summer. There are several varieties, including 'Wirral Supreme' (double) and 'Phyllis Smith' (double, with frilled petals; pictured). It needs fertile, light and well-drained soil.

75–90cm
30–45cm

LIMONIUM PLATYPHYLLUM
SEA LAVENDER
PLUMBAGINACEAE

Also known as *Limonium latifolium* and *Statice latifolia*, this hardy perennial has a somewhat woody base and leathery dark green leaves. From midsummer to early autumn it produces masses of funnel-shaped, lavender-blue flowers. Well-drained soil is essential; avoid those that remain wet during winter.

45–60cm
45cm

LYSIMACHIA PUNCTATA
YELLOW LOOSESTRIFE
PRIMULACEAE

A hardy herbaceous perennial with upright stems that bear cup-shaped bright yellow flowers in whorls up to 20cm (8in) long throughout summer. Clumps eventually form dominant patches of colour. Although it grows in most soils it flourishes in fertile, moisture-retentive but well-drained soil.

60–90cm
38–45cm

SPRING SUMMER AUTUMN WINTER

leaf type   light preference   speed of growth   ease of growth

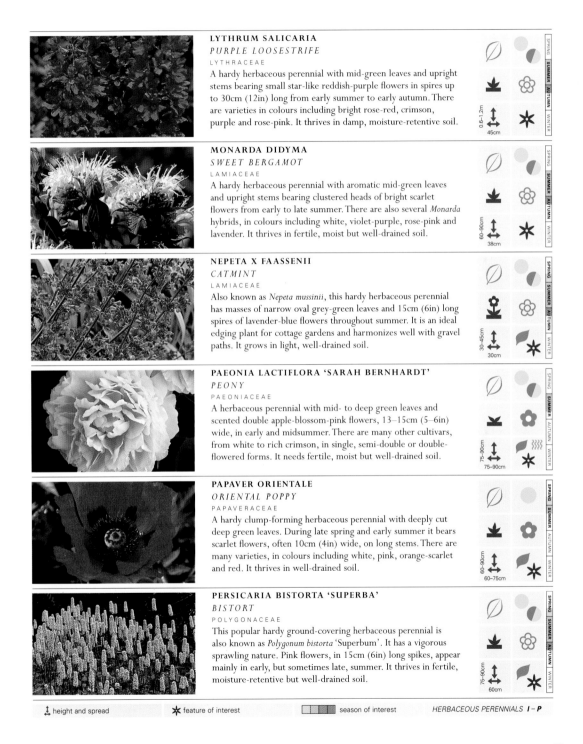

LYTHRUM SALICARIA
PURPLE LOOSESTRIFE
LYTHRACEAE

A hardy herbaceous perennial with mid-green leaves and upright stems bearing small star-like reddish-purple flowers in spires up to 30cm (12in) long from early summer to early autumn. There are varieties in colours including bright rose-red, crimson, purple and rose-pink. It thrives in damp, moisture-retentive soil.

0.6–1.2m
45cm

MONARDA DIDYMA
SWEET BERGAMOT
LAMIACEAE

A hardy herbaceous perennial with aromatic mid-green leaves and upright stems bearing clustered heads of bright scarlet flowers from early to late summer. There are also several *Monarda* hybrids, in colours including white, violet-purple, rose-pink and lavender. It thrives in fertile, moist but well-drained soil.

60–90cm
38cm

NEPETA X FAASSENII
CATMINT
LAMIACEAE

Also known as *Nepeta mussinii*, this hardy herbaceous perennial has masses of narrow oval grey-green leaves and 15cm (6in) long spires of lavender-blue flowers throughout summer. It is an ideal edging plant for cottage gardens and harmonizes well with gravel paths. It grows in light, well-drained soil.

30–45cm
30cm

PAEONIA LACTIFLORA 'SARAH BERNHARDT'
PEONY
PAEONIACEAE

A herbaceous perennial with mid- to deep green leaves and scented double apple-blossom-pink flowers, 13–15cm (5–6in) wide, in early and midsummer. There are many other cultivars, from white to rich crimson, in single, semi-double or double-flowered forms. It needs fertile, moist but well-drained soil.

75–90cm
75–90cm

PAPAVER ORIENTALE
ORIENTAL POPPY
PAPAVERACEAE

A hardy clump-forming herbaceous perennial with deeply cut deep green leaves. During late spring and early summer it bears scarlet flowers, often 10cm (4in) wide, on long stems. There are many varieties, in colours including white, pink, orange-scarlet and red. It thrives in well-drained soil.

60–90cm
60–75cm

PERSICARIA BISTORTA 'SUPERBA'
BISTORT
POLYGONACEAE

This popular hardy ground-covering herbaceous perennial is also known as *Polygonum bistorta* 'Superbum'. It has a vigorous sprawling nature. Pink flowers, in 15cm (6in) long spikes, appear mainly in early, but sometimes late, summer. It thrives in fertile, moisture-retentive but well-drained soil.

75–90cm
60cm

---

height and spread   ✳ feature of interest   ▭▭▭ season of interest   *HERBACEOUS PERENNIALS I – P*

HERBACEOUS PERENNIALS

PHLOX PANICULATA
PHLOX
POLEMONIACEAE

Also known as *Phlox decussata*, this hardy herbaceous perennial bears 10–15cm (4–6in) long clusters of purple flowers from midsummer to autumn. There are several varieties, in violet-blue, salmon-scarlet, pink, bright salmon-orange, claret-red and white. It needs fertile, well-drained but moisture-retentive soil.

0.45–1m
30–45cm

POLYGONATUM X HYBRIDUM
SOLOMON'S SEAL
CONVALLARIACEAE

A popular clump-forming herbaceous perennial with oblong mid-green stem-clasping leaves and pendulous 2.5cm (1in) long white flowers. They are sweetly scented and create a superb feature in a lightly shaded border. It requires fertile, well-drained but moisture-retentive soil.

0.6–1.2m
30–45cm

PULMONARIA OFFICINALIS
LUNGWORT
BORAGINACEAE

A hardy herbaceous perennial with lance-shaped green leaves that reveal white spots. During late spring and early summer it bears purple-blue funnel-shaped flowers. There are several related species, including *Pulmonaria angustifolia* with sky-blue flowers. Moisture-retentive but well-drained soil suits them.

30–38cm
30–38cm

RUDBECKIA FULGIDA VAR. DEAMII
CONEFLOWER
ASTERACEAE

A brightly coloured hardy herbaceous perennial with large daisy-like yellow to orange flowers, each about 6cm (2½in) wide and with a large purple-brown cone-like centre, from midsummer to autumn. There are several other forms, including var. *sullivantii* 'Goldsturm' (also yellow). It needs well-drained soil.

60–90cm
45–60cm

SAPONARIA OFFICINALIS
COMMON SOAPWORT
CARYOPHYLLACEAE

An attractive hardy perennial that sometimes naturalizes itself over large areas. It has sweetly scented single pink salver-shaped flowers with undertones of clover from midsummer to early autumn. It is most often grown in a double-flowered form and thrives in fertile, well-drained but moisture-retentive soil.

30–90cm
45–60cm

SEDUM 'AUTUMN JOY'
ICE PLANT
CRASSULACEAE

Also known as *Sedum spectabile* 'Autumn Joy' and *Sedum* 'Herbstfreude'. It has pale green fleshy leaves and 10–20cm (4–8in) wide heads of salmon-pink flowers that slowly change through orange-red to orange-brown by late autumn. It requires well-drained but moisture-retentive soil.

45–60cm
45–50cm

≣ leaf type   ● light preference   ⚓ speed of growth   ❀ ease of growth

SMILACINA RACEMOSA
FALSE SOLOMON'S SEAL, FALSE SPIKENARD
CONVALLARIACEAE

This hardy herbaceous perennial develops erect stems with light green shiny lance-shaped leaves. Long sprays, about 10cm (4in) long, of sweetly scented creamy white flowers appear at the ends of stems during late spring and early summer. It thrives in fertile, moisture-retentive soil in light shade.

75–90cm
45cm

SPRING SUMMER AUTUMN WINTER

SOLIDAGO 'CROWN OF RAYS'
GOLDEN ROD
ASTERACEAE

A widely grown hardy herbaceous perennial with densely packed plume-like heads of golden-yellow flowers. There are several other superb hybrids, including 'Goldenmosa' (fluffy yellow heads) and 'Queenie' (golden-yellow flowers). They need well-drained but moisture-retentive soil.

45–60cm
30–45cm

SPRING SUMMER AUTUMN WINTER

STACHYS BYZANTINA
LAMB'S TONGUE
LAMIACEAE

A distinctive carpet-forming half-hardy herbaceous perennial that smothers the soil with leaves densely covered in silvery hairs. They have a woolly appearance. During midsummer it develops upright stems that bear spikes of purple flowers. It thrives in well-drained soil, where it spreads to form a clump.

30–45cm
38–45cm

SPRING SUMMER AUTUMN WINTER

THALICTRUM AQUILEGIIFOLIUM
MEADOW RUE
RANUNCULACEAE

A hardy herbaceous perennial with glossy grey-blue leaves and fluffy lilac-pink flowers borne in lax clusters at the tops of tall stems during early and midsummer. There are several superb varieties, in white and shades of purple-mauve. It thrives in rich, moisture-retentive but well-drained soil.

1–1.5m
45–50cm

SPRING SUMMER AUTUMN WINTER

TRADESCANTIA X ANDERSONIANA 'ISIS'
SPIDERWORT
COMMELINACEAE

A distinctive hardy herbaceous perennial with strap-like leaves. From early to late summer it bears rich royal-purple flowers, each about 3.5cm (1⅜in) wide. Other varieties include 'Osprey' (white), 'Purple Dome' (rich purple) and 'J. C. Weguelin' (light blue). It needs moisture-retentive but well-drained soil.

45–60cm
45–50cm

SPRING SUMMER AUTUMN WINTER

TROLLIUS X CULTORUM 'LEMON QUEEN'
GLOBE FLOWER
RANUNCULACEAE

A hardy herbaceous perennial with mid- to deep green leaves. The globe-shaped yellow flowers appear during late spring and early summer. There are many other cultivars, in colours including rich yellow and fiery orange. It is ideal for planting alongside streams and ponds, as well as in moisture-retentive soil in borders.

60–75cm
45cm

SPRING SUMMER AUTUMN WINTER

↕ height and spread   ✳ feature of interest   ▭▭▭ season of interest   *HERBACEOUS PERENNIALS* **P – T**

BULBS, CORMS AND TUBERS

IPHEION UNIFLORUM
SPRING STARFLOWER
ALLIACEAE

A hardy clump-forming bulbous plant with a relaxed nature. It has pale-green grass-like leaves and six-petalled scented white to violet-blue star-like flowers, each 3.5–5cm (1½–2in) wide, in spring. Varieties include 'Wisley Blue' (violet-blue). It requires moisture-retentive but well-drained soil.

15–20cm
10–15cm

CARDIOCRINUM GIGANTEUM
GIANT LILY
LILIACEAE

A hardy bulbous plant with sturdy stems that bear fragrant slightly pendulous cream or greenish-white 15cm (6in) long flowers. The inside of each trumpet is streaked purple or crimson-brown. The dark green leaves are mainly borne in basal rosettes. It needs fertile, moisture-retentive, well-drained soil.

1.8–3m
0.9–1.2m

COLCHICUM 'WATERLILY'
AUTUMN CROCUS
COLCHICACEAE

This hardy cormous hybrid colchicum has a relaxed nature. In autumn it bears large mauve double flowers. The leaves, which appear after the flowers, grow about 23–30cm (9–12in) high. It is ideal for planting in groups within about 60cm (24in) of a path but is poisonous. Needs well-drained, moisture-retentive soil.

15cm
20–25cm

ERANTHIS HYEMALIS
WINTER ACONITE
RANUNCULACEAE

A hardy tuberous-rooted plant with lemon-yellow buttercup-like flowers up to 2.5cm (1in) wide and backed by a ruff of deeply cut light green leaves. During mild seasons they appear in midwinter, but more often during late winter and early spring. It thrives in moisture-retentive but well-drained soil.

10cm
7.5cm

FRITILLARIA IMPERIALIS
CROWN IMPERIAL
LILIACEAE

A hardy bulbous plant with stiff upright stems and clusters of 5cm (2in) long tulip-shaped flowers during mid-spring. Their colours range from yellow to rich red; varieties are available in orange-yellow, lemon-yellow, red and orange-brown. It thrives in fertile, well-drained soil.

60–90cm
23–38cm

HYACINTHOIDES HISPANICA
BLUEBELL
HYACINTHACEAE

Also known as *Endymion hispanicus* and *Scilla hispanica*, this bulbous plant has strap-like glossy-green leaves and upright stems that reveal lax clusters of purple-blue bell-shaped flowers during spring and early summer. There is also a white-flowered form. It needs fertile, moisture-retentive but well-drained soil.

25–30cm
10–13cm

🌿 leaf type   ● light preference   ⚘ speed of growth   ⚘ ease of growth

IPHEION UNIFLORUM
SPRING STARFLOWER
ALLIACEAE

A hardy clump-forming bulbous plant with a relaxed nature. It has pale-green grass-like leaves and six-petalled scented white to violet-blue star-like flowers, each 3.5–5cm (1½–2in) wide, in spring. Varieties include 'Wisley Blue' (violet-blue). It requires moisture-retentive but well-drained soil.

15–20cm
5–7.5cm

LILIUM AURATUM
GOLDEN-RAYED LILY
LILIACEAE

A hardy stem-rooting lily with strongly sweet funnel-shaped brilliant white flowers up to 30cm (12in) wide during late summer and into early autumn. Each flower has gold bands or rays, and purple wine-coloured spots on the inner surface. It thrives in lime-free, well-drained but moisture-retentive soil.

1.5–2.1m
30–38cm

LILIUM CANDIDUM
MADONNA LILY
LILIACEAE

A hardy basal-rooting bulb that develops tall stems with large pure white bell-shaped flowers, 7.5cm (3in) long, during early and midsummer. Each flower has golden anthers at its centre, and exudes a honey-like fragrance. It requires slightly alkaline, well-drained but moisture-retentive soil.

1.2–1.5m
23cm

NARCISSUS
DAFFODILS (LARGE TRUMPET TYPES)
AMARYLLIDACEAE

These popular hardy bulbous plants are well known for their trumpet-shaped flowers, one flower being borne at the top of each stem during spring. There are many varieties, mostly yellow but white and bicoloured varieties are also available. Plant them in fertile, well-drained but moisture-retentive soil.

32–45cm
7.5–10cm

TRILLIUM GRANDIFLORUM 'ROSEUM'
WAKE ROBIN
TRILLIACEAE

A rhizomatous herbaceous clump-forming plant with pale to mid-green leaves. The three-petalled pink flowers have golden anthers and appear in spring and early summer. The species has white flowers, later flushed pink, with golden anthers. It requires fertile, moisture-retentive but well-drained soil.

30–45cm
25–30cm

TULIPA
TULIPS (DOUBLE EARLY)
LILIACEAE

This group of hardy bulbous plants is extremely popular in cottage gardens. The double, spring flowers are up to 10cm (4in) wide. The colour range is wide and includes yellow, pink, violet-purple and orange and red. Plant tulips in slightly chalky, well-drained soil.

30–38cm
15cm

⬍ height and spread ✳ feature of interest ▭▭▭ season of interest *BULBS **A – T***

FERNS

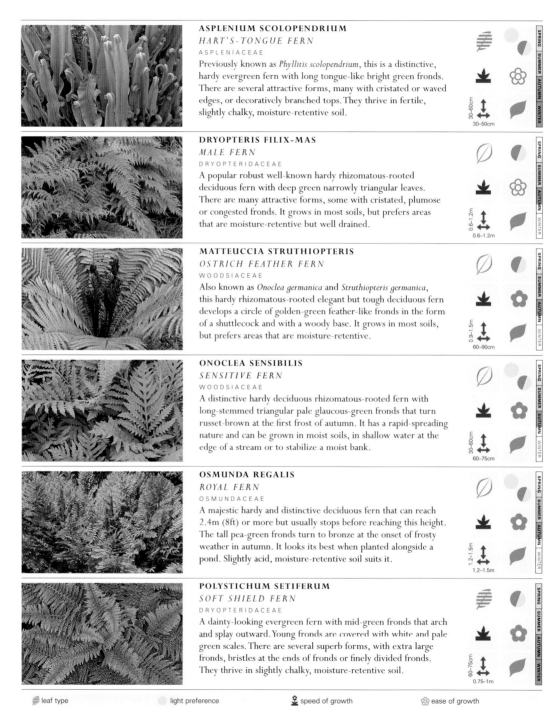

ASPLENIUM SCOLOPENDRIUM
HART'S-TONGUE FERN
ASPLENIACEAE
Previously known as *Phyllitis scolopendrium*, this is a distinctive, hardy evergreen fern with long tongue-like bright green fronds. There are several attractive forms, many with cristated or waved edges, or decoratively branched tops. They thrive in fertile, slightly chalky, moisture-retentive soil.

30–60cm
30–50cm

SPRING SUMMER AUTUMN WINTER

DRYOPTERIS FILIX-MAS
MALE FERN
DRYOPTERIDACEAE
A popular robust well-known hardy rhizomatous-rooted deciduous fern with deep green narrowly triangular leaves. There are many attractive forms, some with cristated, plumose or congested fronds. It grows in most soils, but prefers areas that are moisture-retentive but well drained.

0.6–1.2m
0.6–1.2m

SPRING SUMMER AUTUMN WINTER

MATTEUCCIA STRUTHIOPTERIS
OSTRICH FEATHER FERN
WOODSIACEAE
Also known as *Onoclea germanica* and *Struthiopteris germanica*, this hardy rhizomatous-rooted elegant but tough deciduous fern develops a circle of golden-green feather-like fronds in the form of a shuttlecock and with a woody base. It grows in most soils, but prefers areas that are moisture-retentive.

0.9–1.5m
60–90cm

SPRING SUMMER AUTUMN WINTER

ONOCLEA SENSIBILIS
SENSITIVE FERN
WOODSIACEAE
A distinctive hardy deciduous rhizomatous-rooted fern with long-stemmed triangular pale glaucous-green fronds that turn russet-brown at the first frost of autumn. It has a rapid-spreading nature and can be grown in moist soils, in shallow water at the edge of a stream or to stabilize a moist bank.

30–60cm
60–75cm

SPRING SUMMER AUTUMN WINTER

OSMUNDA REGALIS
ROYAL FERN
OSMUNDACEAE
A majestic hardy and distinctive deciduous fern that can reach 2.4m (8ft) or more but usually stops before reaching this height. The tall pea-green fronds turn to bronze at the onset of frosty weather in autumn. It looks its best when planted alongside a pond. Slightly acid, moisture-retentive soil suits it.

1.2–1.5m
1.2–1.5m

SPRING SUMMER AUTUMN WINTER

POLYSTICHUM SETIFERUM
SOFT SHIELD FERN
DRYOPTERIDACEAE
A dainty-looking evergreen fern with mid-green fronds that arch and splay outward. Young fronds are covered with white and pale green scales. There are several superb forms, with extra large fronds, bristles at the ends of fronds or finely divided fronds. They thrive in slightly chalky, moisture-retentive soil.

60–75cm
0.75–1m

SPRING SUMMER AUTUMN WINTER

leaf type   light preference   speed of growth   ease of growth

GRASSES

COIX LACRYMA-JOBI
JOB'S TEARS
POACEAE

A distinctive tufted half-hardy annual grass with broad somewhat lance-shaped pale to mid-green leaves borne on arching stems. From midsummer to early autumn it bears woody grey-green edible seeds that hang in tear-like clusters. It thrives in fertile, moisture-retentive but well-drained soil.

45–60cm
23cm

FESTUCA GLAUCA
BLUE FESCUE
POACEAE

A hardy perennial with narrow bristle-like blue-grey leaves. During early and midsummer it bears purple spikelets on stems about 30cm (12in) long. There are several varieties, some dwarf but most with coloured leaves, including silvery-blue, blue-green and blue. It thrives in light, well-drained soil.

15–23cm
15–23cm

HOLCUS MOLLIS 'ALBOVARIEGATUS'
VARIEGATED CREEPING SOFT GRASS
POACEAE

This hardy perennial grass is a cultivar of the somewhat invasive creeping soft grass. This variegated form, however, is more attractive and has leaves striped alternately silver and grey-green. Incidentally, plants raised from seeds are not variegated. Plant it in neutral or slightly acid light soil.

30–45cm
30–38cm

MISCANTHUS SINENSIS 'VARIEGATUS'
JAPANESE VARIEGATED SILVER GRASS
POACEAE

A hardy rhizomatous-rooted clump-forming perennial with rigid erect green leaves variegated creamy-white. There are many other varieties, including 'Zebrinus' (zebra grass) with irregular yellow crossbanding on a green background. Plant it in light, moisture-retentive soil.

0.9–1.2m
45–60cm

PENNISETUM VILLOSUM
FEATHER GRASS
POACEAE

Also known as *Pennisetum longistylum*, this half-hardy perennial is usually grown as a half-hardy annual. It has narrow mid-green arching leaves and hairy stems. During early and midsummer it bears white, sometimes tawny-brown to purple, flowers. It needs light, well-drained but moisture-retentive soil.

45–60cm
30cm

PHALARIS ARUNDINACEA VAR. PICTA
GARDENERS' GARTERS
POACEAE

A distinctive hardy perennial grass with a lax nature and rhizomatous spreading roots. It develops narrow leaf blades with cream and bright green longitudinal stripes. The lower leaves tend to arch, while the central ones are more upright. Plant it in well-drained, but not excessively rich, soil.

60cm
45–60cm

⬍ height and spread   ✳ feature of interest   ▭▭▭ season of interest   *FERNS AND GRASSES* **A – P**

SHRUBS

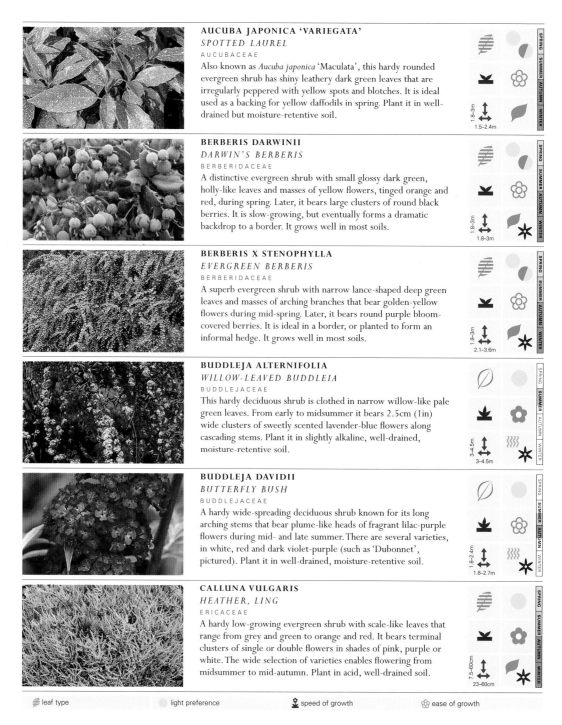

AUCUBA JAPONICA 'VARIEGATA'
SPOTTED LAUREL
AUCUBACEAE

Also known as *Aucuba japonica* 'Maculata', this hardy rounded evergreen shrub has shiny leathery dark green leaves that are irregularly peppered with yellow spots and blotches. It is ideal used as a backing for yellow daffodils in spring. Plant it in well-drained but moisture-retentive soil.

1.8–3m
1.5–2.4m

BERBERIS DARWINII
DARWIN'S BERBERIS
BERBERIDACEAE

A distinctive evergreen shrub with small glossy dark green, holly-like leaves and masses of yellow flowers, tinged orange and red, during spring. Later, it bears large clusters of round black berries. It is slow-growing, but eventually forms a dramatic backdrop to a border. It grows well in most soils.

1.8–3m
1.8–3m

BERBERIS X STENOPHYLLA
EVERGREEN BERBERIS
BERBERIDACEAE

A superb evergreen shrub with narrow lance-shaped deep green leaves and masses of arching branches that bear golden-yellow flowers during mid-spring. Later, it bears round purple bloom-covered berries. It is ideal in a border, or planted to form an informal hedge. It grows well in most soils.

1.8–3m
2.1–3.6m

BUDDLEJA ALTERNIFOLIA
WILLOW-LEAVED BUDDLEIA
BUDDLEJACEAE

This hardy deciduous shrub is clothed in narrow willow-like pale green leaves. From early to midsummer it bears 2.5cm (1in) wide clusters of sweetly scented lavender-blue flowers along cascading stems. Plant it in slightly alkaline, well-drained, moisture-retentive soil.

3–4.5m
3–4.5m

BUDDLEJA DAVIDII
BUTTERFLY BUSH
BUDDLEJACEAE

A hardy wide-spreading deciduous shrub known for its long arching stems that bear plume-like heads of fragrant lilac-purple flowers during mid- and late summer. There are several varieties, in white, red and dark violet-purple (such as 'Dubonnet', pictured). Plant it in well-drained, moisture-retentive soil.

1.8–2.4m
1.8–2.7m

CALLUNA VULGARIS
HEATHER, LING
ERICACEAE

A hardy low-growing evergreen shrub with scale-like leaves that range from grey and green to orange and red. It bears terminal clusters of single or double flowers in shades of pink, purple or white. The wide selection of varieties enables flowering from midsummer to mid-autumn. Plant in acid, well-drained soil.

7.5–60cm
23–60cm

SPRING | SUMMER | AUTUMN | WINTER

🌿 leaf type   ⬤ light preference   🌱 speed of growth   ✿ ease of growth

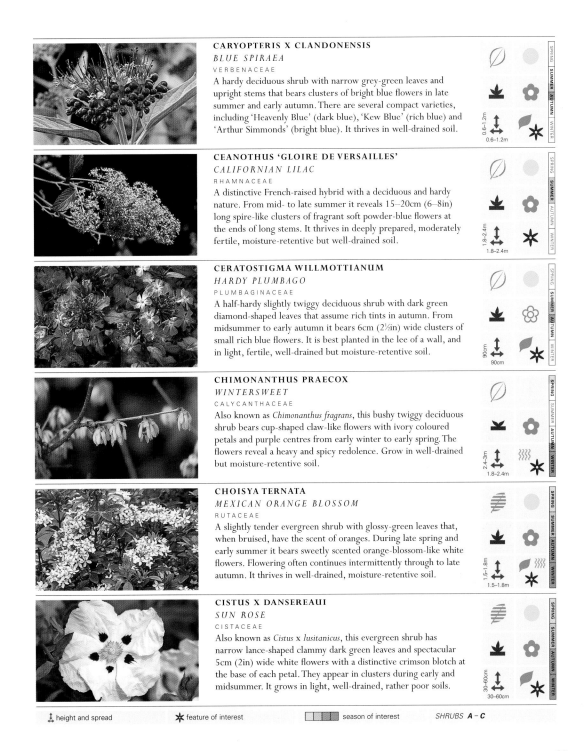

CARYOPTERIS X CLANDONENSIS
BLUE SPIRAEA
VERBENACEAE

A hardy deciduous shrub with narrow grey-green leaves and upright stems that bears clusters of bright blue flowers in late summer and early autumn. There are several compact varieties, including 'Heavenly Blue' (dark blue), 'Kew Blue' (rich blue) and 'Arthur Simmonds' (bright blue). It thrives in well-drained soil.

0.6–1.2m
0.6–1.2m

SPRING SUMMER AUTUMN WINTER

CEANOTHUS 'GLOIRE DE VERSAILLES'
CALIFORNIAN LILAC
RHAMNACEAE

A distinctive French-raised hybrid with a deciduous and hardy nature. From mid- to late summer it reveals 15–20cm (6–8in) long spire-like clusters of fragrant soft powder-blue flowers at the ends of long stems. It thrives in deeply prepared, moderately fertile, moisture-retentive but well-drained soil.

1.8–2.4m
1.8–2.4m

SPRING SUMMER AUTUMN WINTER

CERATOSTIGMA WILLMOTTIANUM
HARDY PLUMBAGO
PLUMBAGINACEAE

A half-hardy slightly twiggy deciduous shrub with dark green diamond-shaped leaves that assume rich tints in autumn. From midsummer to early autumn it bears 6cm (2½in) wide clusters of small rich blue flowers. It is best planted in the lee of a wall, and in light, fertile, well-drained but moisture-retentive soil.

90cm
90cm

SPRING SUMMER AUTUMN WINTER

CHIMONANTHUS PRAECOX
WINTERSWEET
CALYCANTHACEAE

Also known as *Chimonanthus fragrans*, this bushy twiggy deciduous shrub bears cup-shaped claw-like flowers with ivory coloured petals and purple centres from early winter to early spring. The flowers reveal a heavy and spicy redolence. Grow in well-drained but moisture-retentive soil.

2.4–3m
1.8–2.4m

SPRING SUMMER AUTUMN WINTER

CHOISYA TERNATA
MEXICAN ORANGE BLOSSOM
RUTACEAE

A slightly tender evergreen shrub with glossy-green leaves that, when bruised, have the scent of oranges. During late spring and early summer it bears sweetly scented orange-blossom-like white flowers. Flowering often continues intermittently through to late autumn. It thrives in well-drained, moisture-retentive soil.

1.5–1.8m
1.5–1.8m

SPRING SUMMER AUTUMN WINTER

CISTUS X DANSEREAUI
SUN ROSE
CISTACEAE

Also known as *Cistus* x *lusitanicus*, this evergreen shrub has narrow lance-shaped clammy dark green leaves and spectacular 5cm (2in) wide white flowers with a distinctive crimson blotch at the base of each petal. They appear in clusters during early and midsummer. It grows in light, well-drained, rather poor soils.

30–60cm
30–60cm

SPRING SUMMER AUTUMN WINTER

⸸ height and spread   ✳ feature of interest   ▭▭▭▭ season of interest   *SHRUBS* **A – C**

SHRUBS

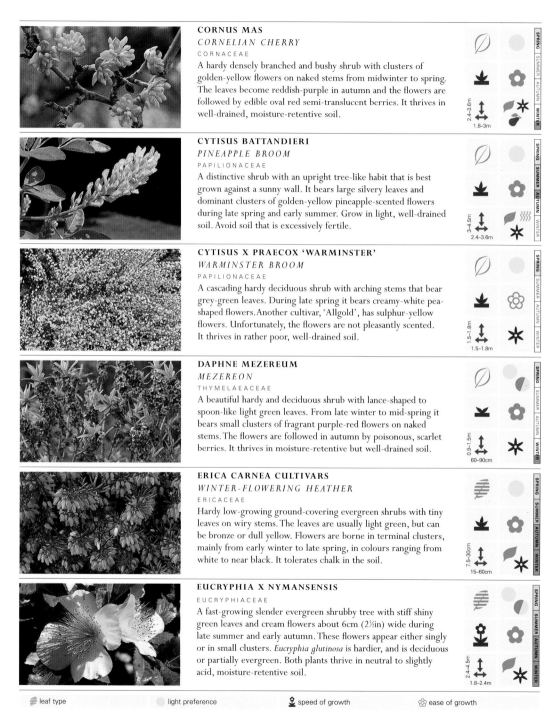

CORNUS MAS
CORNELIAN CHERRY
CORNACEAE

A hardy densely branched and bushy shrub with clusters of
golden-yellow flowers on naked stems from midwinter to spring.
The leaves become reddish-purple in autumn and the flowers are
followed by edible oval red semi-translucent berries. It thrives in
well-drained, moisture-retentive soil.

2.4–3.6m
1.8–3m

CYTISUS BATTANDIERI
PINEAPPLE BROOM
PAPILIONACEAE

A distinctive shrub with an upright tree-like habit that is best
grown against a sunny wall. It bears large silvery leaves and
dominant clusters of golden-yellow pineapple-scented flowers
during late spring and early summer. Grow in light, well-drained
soil. Avoid soil that is excessively fertile.

3–4.5m
2.4–3.6m

CYTISUS X PRAECOX 'WARMINSTER'
WARMINSTER BROOM
PAPILIONACEAE

A cascading hardy deciduous shrub with arching stems that bear
grey-green leaves. During late spring it bears creamy-white pea-
shaped flowers. Another cultivar, 'Allgold', has sulphur-yellow
flowers. Unfortunately, the flowers are not pleasantly scented.
It thrives in rather poor, well-drained soil.

1.5–1.8m
1.5–1.8m

DAPHNE MEZEREUM
MEZEREON
THYMELAEACEAE

A beautiful hardy and deciduous shrub with lance-shaped to
spoon-like light green leaves. From late winter to mid-spring it
bears small clusters of fragrant purple-red flowers on naked
stems. The flowers are followed in autumn by poisonous, scarlet
berries. It thrives in moisture-retentive but well-drained soil.

0.9–1.5m
60–90cm

ERICA CARNEA CULTIVARS
WINTER-FLOWERING HEATHER
ERICACEAE

Hardy low-growing ground-covering evergreen shrubs with tiny
leaves on wiry stems. The leaves are usually light green, but can
be bronze or dull yellow. Flowers are borne in terminal clusters,
mainly from early winter to late spring, in colours ranging from
white to near black. It tolerates chalk in the soil.

7.5–30cm
15–60cm

EUCRYPHIA X NYMANSENSIS
EUCRYPHIACEAE

A fast-growing slender evergreen shrubby tree with stiff shiny
green leaves and cream flowers about 6cm (2⅜in) wide during
late summer and early autumn. These flowers appear either singly
or in small clusters. *Eucryphia glutinosa* is hardier, and is deciduous
or partially evergreen. Both plants thrive in neutral to slightly
acid, moisture-retentive soil.

2.4–4.5m
1.8–2.4m

SPRING | SUMMER | AUTUMN | WINTER

🍃 leaf type   ● light preference   ⚓ speed of growth   ✿ ease of growth

EUONYMUS JAPONICUS 'DUC D'ANJOU'

CELASTRACEAE

This hardy bushy evergreen shrub has broadly lance-shaped dark green leaves variegated yellow and green. It is best grown in sheltered areas and is ideal for planting near the coast where it will thrive. There are many other varieties with attractively variegated leaves. Plant all of these in well-drained soil.

60–90cm
0.75–1.2m

SPRING SUMMER AUTUMN WINTER

FORSYTHIA X INTERMEDIA

GOLDEN BELLS

OLEACEAE

A popular hardy and widely grown deciduous shrub with masses of golden-yellow bell-shaped flowers, each about 2.5cm (1in) wide, during mid- and late spring. Varieties include 'Spectabilis' (bright yellow) and 'Lynwood' (large, rich yellow). It thrives in fertile, moisture-retentive but well-drained soil.

1.8–2.4m
2.1–2.4m

SPRING SUMMER AUTUMN WINTER

FUCHSIA MAGELLANICA

LADY'S EARDROPS

ONAGRACEAE

A slightly tender herbaceous bushy and spreading shrub with lance-shaped mid-green leaves and pendent crimson and purple flowers, each up to 5cm (2in) long, from midsummer to autumn. Although tender, it is the hardiest of garden fuchsias and thrives in light, well-drained but moisture-retentive soil.

1.2–1.8m
0.6–1.2m

SPRING SUMMER AUTUMN WINTER

GENISTA CINEREA

BROOM

PAPILIONACEAE

A hardy deciduous slender-stemmed shrub with small grey-green leaves and slightly arching stems that bear a profusion of sweetly scented yellow flowers in loose terminal clusters during early and midsummer. After the flowers fade it develops silky seed pods. It thrives in light, well-drained, rather poor soil.

2.4–3m
1.8–2.4m

SPRING SUMMER AUTUMN WINTER

GENISTA HISPANICA

SPANISH GORSE

PAPILIONACEAE

A spreading densely branched hardy deciduous shrub with spine-clustered stems. During early and midsummer it bears masses of deep yellow flowers in 2.5cm (1in) wide terminal clusters. When in flower, its strong colouring tends to dominate nearby plants. It thrives in light, well-drained, rather poor soil.

0.6–1.2m
1.5–2.4m

SPRING SUMMER AUTUMN WINTER

HEBE 'AUTUMN GLORY'

SHRUBBY VERONICA

SCROPHULARIACEAE

A hardy sparsely branched and erect evergreen shrub with purple stems bearing glossy green leaves edged red when young. Spikes of deep purplish-blue flowers appear from midsummer to autumn. There are several other hybrids, including 'Midsummer Beauty' (lavender-purple). It thrives in well-drained soil.

60–90cm
60–90cm

SPRING SUMMER AUTUMN WINTER

⊥ height and spread   ✳ feature of interest   ▭▭▭▭ season of interest   *SHRUBS C – H*

SHRUBS

HELICHRYSUM ITALICUM
CURRY PLANT
ASTERACEAE

Also known as *Helichrysum angustifolium*, this deciduous shrub is famed for the curry-like redolence of its silvery-grey down-covered leaves. From early to late summer it reveals masses of small mustard-yellow flowers borne in clusters up to 5cm (2in) wide. It thrives in light, well-drained soil.

23–45cm
45–60cm

HIBISCUS SYRIACUS
SHRUBBY MALLOW
MALVACEAE

A hardy deciduous shrub with a bushy upright nature and rich green three-lobed coarsely tooth-edged leaves. From mid-summer to early autumn it reveals 7.5cm (3in) wide flowers in colours including rose-pink, violet-blue and white with red centres. Grow in fertile, well-drained, moisture-retentive soil.

1.8–3m
1.2–1.8m

HYDRANGEA ARBORESCENS
TREE HYDRANGEA
HYDRANGEACEAE

A hardy deciduous shrub with bright green leaves and slightly domed heads, up to 15cm (6in) wide, with dull white flowers during mid- and late summer — or later. As the season progresses they turn bronze-brown. 'Grandiflora' has larger flowers. It thrives in fertile, moisture-retentive, well-drained soil.

1.2–1.8m
1.2–1.8m

HYDRANGEA MACROPHYLLA
HYDRANGEA
HYDRANGEACEAE

A midsummer- to autumn-flowering hardy shrub. Hortensia types (shown) have mop-like pink to blue flower heads, 13–20cm (5–8in) wide. Lacecap types bear flat heads, 10–15cm (4–6in) wide. It thrives in fertile, moisture-retentive, well-drained soil. The soil's acidity or alkalinity influences the flower's colour.

1.2–1.8m
1.5–2.1m

HYPERICUM 'HIDCOTE'
ROSE OF SHARON
CLUSIACEAE

Also known as *Hypericum patulum* 'Hidcote', this bushy shrub has an almost evergreen nature. From midsummer to early autumn it bears large saucer-shaped waxy golden-yellow flowers, each about 7.5cm (3in) wide. It thrives in fertile, moisture-retentive but well-drained soil. Avoid dry soil.

1.2–1.5m
1.5–2.1m

KERRIA JAPONICA 'PLENIFLORA'
BACHELOR'S BUTTONS
ROSACEAE

A lax hardy deciduous shrub with slender glossy green stems and bright green tooth-edged leaves. During late spring and into early summer it develops double orange-yellow flowers about 5cm (2in) wide. Another cultivar, 'Picta', has leaves edged in white. It thrives in well-drained but moisture-retentive soil.

1.8–2.4m
1.5–2.1m

SPRING · SUMMER · AUTUMN · WINTER

🌿 leaf type   ● light preference   ⚓ speed of growth   ✿ ease of growth

KOLKWITZIA AMABILIS
BEAUTY BUSH
CAPRIFOLIACEAE

A hardy deciduous shrub with a twiggy nature and arching branches bearing dark green leaves. The stems have peeling brown bark. During late spring and early summer it is covered with pink foxglove-like flowers with yellow throats. Plant it in well-drained but moisture-retentive soil.

1.8–3m
1.5–2.4m

LAVATERA 'ROSEA'
TREE MALLOW
MALVACEAE

Also known as *Lavatera olbia* 'Rosea', it has a relaxed cottage-garden nature, with soft stems bearing large three- to five-lobed grey-green leaves. Masses of rose-coloured 6cm (2½in) wide flowers appear from midsummer to autumn. It thrives in light, well-drained but moisture-retentive soil.

1.5–2.1m
1.8–2.4m

MAHONIA X MEDIA 'CHARITY'
BERBERIDACEAE

Also known as *Mahonia* 'Charity', this hardy evergreen shrub has leathery, mid- to dark green leaves formed of up to 21 spiny leaflets. From early to late winter it bears 23–30cm (9–12in) long spires of fragrant deep lemon-yellow flowers. The plant needs moisture-retentive but well-drained soil, which it prefers to be slightly acidic.

1.8–2.4m
1.5–2.1m

PHILADELPHUS CORONARIUS 'AUREUS'
GOLDEN-LEAVED MOCK ORANGE
HYDRANGEACEAE

A hardy shrub with an upright stance and orange-blossom-scented creamy-white flowers during early and midsummer. It is best known for its golden-yellow leaves, which slowly become greenish-yellow as summer progresses. It thrives in most soils, but especially in fertile, moisture-retentive, well-drained types.

1.5–2.1m
1.5–1.8m

PHILADELPHUS HYBRIDS
MOCK ORANGE
HYDRANGEACEAE

These hardy bushy deciduous shrubs are popular and widely grown. During early and midsummer they bear single or double white cup-shaped scented flowers. Varieties range in height and spread. They thrive in most soil, but especially in fertile, moisture-retentive, well-drained types.

0.9–3m
0.9–3.6m

POTENTILLA FRUTICOSA
SHRUBBY CINQUEFOIL
ROSACEAE

A deciduous shrub with mid-green leaves and buttercup-yellow saucer-shaped flowers, each 2.5cm (1in) wide, from early to late summer – and sometimes later. There are several varieties, in white, glowing red, orange to brick-red and tangerine-red. It thrives in light, well-drained but moisture-retentive soil.

1.2–1.5m
1.2–1.5m

---

height and spread   feature of interest   season of interest   *SHRUBS* **H – P**

SHRUBS

RHODODENDRON LUTEUM

ERICACEAE

Also known as *Azalea luteum*, this hardy deciduous shrub has a lax nature and large clusters of sweetly fragrant rich yellow flowers during spring and early summer. In autumn the leaves assume rich scarlet shades. It is an ideal plant for placing along the top of a low bank bordering a stream. It requires fertile, light, slightly acid and moisture-retentive soil.

1.8–3m
1.5–2m

ROMNEYA COULTERI VAR. TRICHOCALYX

TREE POPPY

PAPAVERACEAE

A hardy semi-woody shrub with herbaceous-like stems and deeply lobed blue-green leaves. From mid- to late summer, sometimes later, it bears slightly fragrant white poppy-like flowers up to 13cm (5in) wide. It thrives in fertile, deeply prepared, well-drained, moisture-retentive soil.

0.9–1.2m
0.9–1.2m

SARCOCOCCA HUMILIS

CHRISTMAS BOX

BUXACEAE

Also known as *Sarcococca hookeriana* var. *humilis*, this dwarf suckering densely branched evergreen shrub has lance-shaped dark green leaves. These bear clusters of sweetly scented white flowers during late winter and early spring. Later, it has reddish-black berries. Plant it in well-drained soil; it likes chalky situations.

45–60cm
60–90cm

SPARTIUM JUNCEUM

SPANISH BROOM

PAPILIONACEAE

A hardy deciduous shrub with green rush-like stems that create an evergreen appearance. During summer the stems are covered with narrow mid-green leaves, while from early to late summer it bears fragrant pea-shaped golden-yellow flowers in terminal clusters. Grow in well-drained soil.

1.8–2.4m
1.5–2.1m

SPIRAEA X ARGUTA

FOAM OF MAY

ROSACEAE

A hardy bushy dense twiggy deciduous shrub with narrowly lance-shaped mid-green leaves. During spring the slender branches are drenched in pure white flowers in clusters up to 5cm (2in) wide. It thrives in fertile, deeply prepared, moisture-retentive but well-drained soil.

1.8–2.4m
1.5–2.1m

SYRINGA MEYERI 'PALIBIN'

LILAC

OLEACEAE

A hardy bushy rounded small-leaved lilac that is ideal for a small cottage garden. It has oval dark green leaves and violet-purple flowers borne in small rounded clusters up to 10cm (4in) long during early summer. It thrives in fertile, deeply prepared, moisture-retentive but well-drained soil.

1.5–1.8m
1.5m

leaf type   light preference   speed of growth   ease of growth

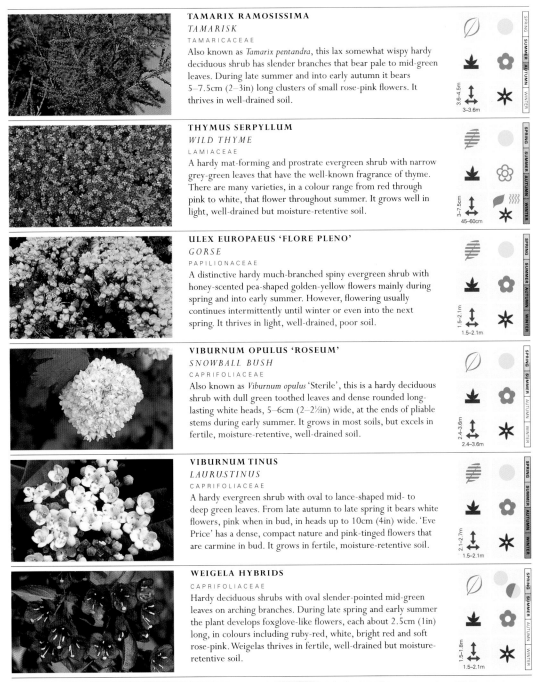

TAMARIX RAMOSISSIMA
TAMARISK
TAMARICACEAE

Also known as *Tamarix pentandra*, this lax somewhat wispy hardy deciduous shrub has slender branches that bear pale to mid-green leaves. During late summer and into early autumn it bears 5–7.5cm (2–3in) long clusters of small rose-pink flowers. It thrives in well-drained soil.

3.6–4.5m
3–3.6m

THYMUS SERPYLLUM
WILD THYME
LAMIACEAE

A hardy mat-forming and prostrate evergreen shrub with narrow grey-green leaves that have the well-known fragrance of thyme. There are many varieties, in a colour range from red through pink to white, that flower throughout summer. It grows well in light, well-drained but moisture-retentive soil.

3–7.5cm
45–60cm

ULEX EUROPAEUS 'FLORE PLENO'
GORSE
PAPILIONACEAE

A distinctive hardy much-branched spiny evergreen shrub with honey-scented pea-shaped golden-yellow flowers mainly during spring and into early summer. However, flowering usually continues intermittently until winter or even into the next spring. It thrives in light, well-drained, poor soil.

1.5–2.1m
1.5–2.1m

VIBURNUM OPULUS 'ROSEUM'
SNOWBALL BUSH
CAPRIFOLIACEAE

Also known as *Viburnum opulus* 'Sterile', this is a hardy deciduous shrub with dull green toothed leaves and dense rounded long-lasting white heads, 5–6cm (2–2⅓in) wide, at the ends of pliable stems during early summer. It grows in most soils, but excels in fertile, moisture-retentive, well-drained soil.

2.4–3.6m
2.4–3.6m

VIBURNUM TINUS
LAURUSTINUS
CAPRIFOLIACEAE

A hardy evergreen shrub with oval to lance-shaped mid- to deep green leaves. From late autumn to late spring it bears white flowers, pink when in bud, in heads up to 10cm (4in) wide. 'Eve Price' has a dense, compact nature and pink-tinged flowers that are carmine in bud. It grows in fertile, moisture-retentive soil.

2.1–2.7m
1.5–2.1m

WEIGELA HYBRIDS
CAPRIFOLIACEAE

Hardy deciduous shrubs with oval slender-pointed mid-green leaves on arching branches. During late spring and early summer the plant develops foxglove-like flowers, each about 2.5cm (1in) long, in colours including ruby-red, white, bright red and soft rose-pink. Weigelas thrives in fertile, well-drained but moisture-retentive soil.

1.5–1.8m
1.5–2.1m

⬍ height and spread   ✳ feature of interest   ▭▭▭ season of interest   *SHRUBS* **R – W**

TREES

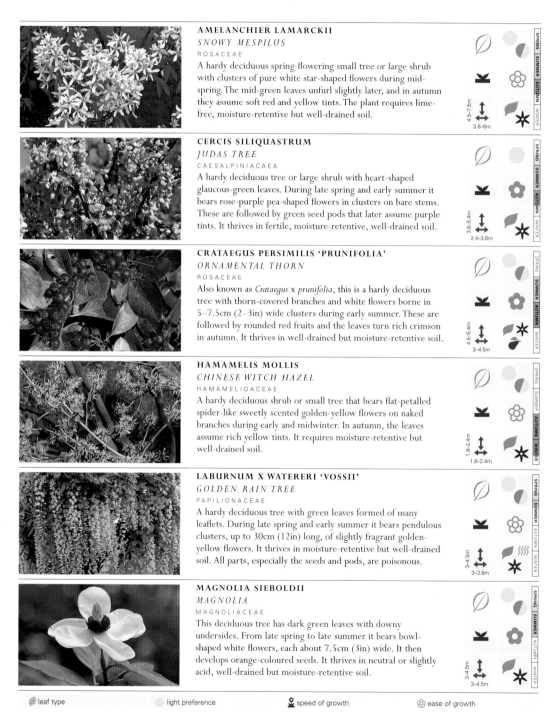

AMELANCHIER LAMARCKII
SNOWY MESPILUS
ROSACEAE

A hardy deciduous spring-flowering small tree or large shrub with clusters of pure white star-shaped flowers during mid-spring. The mid-green leaves unfurl slightly later, and in autumn they assume soft red and yellow tints. The plant requires lime-free, moisture-retentive but well-drained soil.

4.5–7.5m
3.6–6m

CERCIS SILIQUASTRUM
JUDAS TREE
CAESALPINIACEA

A hardy deciduous tree or large shrub with heart-shaped glaucous-green leaves. During late spring and early summer it bears rose-purple pea-shaped flowers in clusters on bare stems. These are followed by green seed pods that later assume purple tints. It thrives in fertile, moisture-retentive, well-drained soil.

3.6–5.4m
2.4–3.6m

CRATAEGUS PERSIMILIS 'PRUNIFOLIA'
ORNAMENTAL THORN
ROSACEAE

Also known as *Crataegus* x *prunifolia*, this is a hardy deciduous tree with thorn-covered branches and white flowers borne in 5–7.5cm (2–3in) wide clusters during early summer. These are followed by rounded red fruits and the leaves turn rich crimson in autumn. It thrives in well-drained but moisture-retentive soil.

4.5–5.4m
3–4.5m

HAMAMELIS MOLLIS
CHINESE WITCH HAZEL
HAMAMELIDACEAE

A hardy deciduous shrub or small tree that bears flat-petalled spider-like sweetly scented golden-yellow flowers on naked branches during early and midwinter. In autumn, the leaves assume rich yellow tints. It requires moisture-retentive but well-drained soil.

1.8–2.4m
1.8–2.4m

LABURNUM X WATERERI 'VOSSII'
GOLDEN RAIN TREE
PAPILIONACEAE

A hardy deciduous tree with green leaves formed of many leaflets. During late spring and early summer it bears pendulous clusters, up to 30cm (12in) long, of slightly fragrant golden-yellow flowers. It thrives in moisture-retentive but well-drained soil. All parts, especially the seeds and pods, are poisonous.

3–4m
3–3.6m

MAGNOLIA SIEBOLDII
MAGNOLIA
MAGNOLIACEAE

This deciduous tree has dark green leaves with downy undersides. From late spring to late summer it bears bowl-shaped white flowers, each about 7.5cm (3in) wide. It then develops orange-coloured seeds. It thrives in neutral or slightly acid, well-drained but moisture-retentive soil.

3–4.5m
3–4.5m

SPRING | SUMMER | AUTUMN | WINTER

🌿 leaf type   ⬤ light preference   ♟ speed of growth   🏵 ease of growth

MAGNOLIA STELLATA
STAR MAGNOLIA
MAGNOLIACEAE

A hardy slow-growing deciduous tree with a compact and rounded nature. During early and mid-spring it bears star-shaped, 7.5–10cm (3–4in) wide white fragrant flowers. Later, it develops lance-shaped pale to mid-green leaves. It requires well-drained but moisture-retentive soil.

2.4–3m
2.4–3m

MALUS X PURPUREA 'ELEYI'
ORNAMENTAL CRAB APPLE
ROSACEAE

A hardy deciduous tree with oval, finely toothed dark red to purple leaves and clusters of single 2.5cm (1in) wide deep reddish-purple flowers in apple-blossom-like clusters during mid-spring. In autumn it bears purplish-red, conical fruits, and thrives in fertile, moisture-retentive but well-drained soil.

5.4–6m
4.5–6m

PRUNUS 'ACCOLADE'
CHERRY
ROSACEAE

A hardy graceful deciduous open and spreading tree with masses of deep blush-pink semi-double flowers that are deep rosy-pink when in bud. These flowers are borne in pendulous clusters during early and mid-spring. It thrives in well-drained but moisture-retentive, slightly alkaline soil.

4.5–6m
4.5–7.5m

PRUNUS PADUS 'WATERERI'
BIRD CHERRY
ROSACEAE

Also known as *Prunus padus* 'Grandiflora', this hardy deciduous tree with spreading branches bears dark-green leaves. During late spring – and sometimes into early summer – it reveals 20cm (8in) long tassels packed with white almond-scented flowers. It thrives in slightly alkaline, well-drained, moisture-retentive soil.

6–7.5m
4.5–6m

PRUNUS PENDULA 'PENDULA ROSEA'
WEEPING SPRING CHERRY
ROSACEAE

Also known as *Prunus* x *subhirtella* 'Pendula', this hardy spreading deciduous tree creates a distinctive feature during spring, when it reveals pendulous branches bearing pale pink flowers. It is superb when underplanted with yellow daffodils. It thrives in slightly alkaline, well-drained, moisture-retentive soil.

3.6–4.5m
3–6m

PRUNUS 'TAIHAKU'
GREAT WHITE CHERRY
ROSACEAE

A hardy vigorous deciduous tree that during mid-spring bears pure white single saucer-shaped flowers. The flowers create a superb colour contrast with the young rich copper-red leaves. In autumn, these leaves assume yellow and orange tints. It thrives in slightly alkaline, well-drained but moisture-retentive soil.

6–7.5m
4.5–7.5m

↨ height and spread   ✳ feature of interest   ▮▮▮▮ season of interest   *TREES* **A – P**

SHRUB AND SPECIES ROSES

ROSA 'ABRAHAM DARBY'
ROSACEAE

A New English rose with large deeply cupped blooms in shades of yellow and apricot during early summer and repeating later. They have a rich fruit-like fragrance. The shiny leaves are attractive and the plant is resistant to diseases. It forms a superb shrub for display on its own or as a background for smaller plants and thrives in well-drained, moisture-retentive soil.

1.5m
1.5m

ROSA 'BUFF BEAUTY'
ROSACEAE

This Hybrid Musk rose has a deciduous nature and bears large trusses of medium-size petal-packed warm apricot-yellow flowers with the bouquet of freshly opened packets of tea combined with a slightly tarry redolence. These are borne amid luxuriant dark green leaves. It thrives in well-drained but moisture-retentive soil.

1.5m
1.5m

ROSA 'FRITZ NOBIS'
ROSACEAE

A Modern Shrub rose with a bushy deciduous nature. It has a relaxed cottage-garden habit, with attractively scrolled buds that resemble those of Hybrid Tea roses. The flowers are a delicate fresh pink with darker shading and have the fragrance of cloves. In the autumn it reveals attractive fruits, widely known as hips or heps. It requires well-drained but moisture-retentive soil.

1.2–1.5m
1.5–1.8m

ROSA GALLICA 'VERSICOLOR'
ROSACEAE

This bushy deciduous Shrub rose, also known as *Rosa mundi*, is a sport from *Rosa gallica* var. *officinalis*, the well-known Apothecary's rose. It has a thicket-forming and suckering nature, with showy semi-double, fragrant deep pink to light crimson flowers striped blush to white. Plant it in well-drained but moisture-retentive soil.

1.2m
0.9–1.2m

ROSA 'HERITAGE'
ROSACEAE

A New English rose with medium-sized cupped clear shell-pink flowers during early summer and with a repeat-flowering nature. The fragrance is exquisite, having the overtones of lemon combined with the scent of an Old rose. This rose is also suitable as a small climber and it requires well-drained but moisture-retentive soil.

1.2m
1.2m

ROSA 'MADAME HARDY'
ROSACEAE

A Damask rose with medium-sized cupped white flowers that have a lemon-like fragrance. When fully open the flowers are quartered and reveal small green centres. The inner petals remain incurved, while the outer ones turn down. Flowering is mainly during midsummer. Plant it in well-drained but moisture-retentive soil.

1.8m
1.5m

leaf type   light preference   speed of growth   ease of growth

ROSA 'MADAME ISAAC PEREIRE'

ROSACEAE

A Bourbon rose with a bushy nature. During early summer and recurrently through to late summer it bears large richly fragrant madder-crimson cupped and quartered, later reflexing, flowers. It can also be grown as a climber, when it reaches 2.4–2.7m (8–9ft) high. Plant it in well-drained but moisture-retentive soil.

1.5m
1.2m

ROSA 'NEVADA'

ROSACEAE

This Modern Shrub rose has a bushy deciduous nature and semi-double 10cm (4in) wide slightly fragrant creamy-white flowers with yellow stamens during early and midsummer. The plant also has the bonus of thornless reddish-brown arching stems and small light green leaves. Plant it in well-drained but moisture-retentive soil.

1.8–2.1m
1.8–2.1m

ROSA 'ROSY CUSHION'

ROSACEAE

This Modern Shrub rose is ideal for covering the ground with colour. It also works well planted between roses that are grown as standards (on tall stems). It has a deciduous nature and large clusters of slightly fragrant semi-double pink flowers with white centres, mainly during early summer but with a repeat-flowering nature. It requires well-drained but moisture-retentive soil.

75cm
1.2–1.5m

ROSA RUBIGINOSA

SWEET BRIAR
ROSACEAE

Also known as *Rosa eglanteria*, this deciduous species rose has an erect and arching nature. Prickly stems bear leaves that reveal a strong fragrance. Single bright pink flowers, about 3.5cm (1⅜in) wide, appear during early summer, followed by orange-red fruits. It thrives in well-drained, moisture-retentive soil.

1.8–2.1m
1.8–2.4m

ROSA 'SARAH VAN FLEET'

ROSACEAE

A superb sturdy and robust Shrub rose, with an upright, bushy and deciduous nature. From early to late summer it bears fragrant large slightly cupped and double clear mallow-pink flowers with creamy-yellow stamens. The flowers are borne amid light green wrinkled leaves and it thrives in well-drained but moisture-retentive soil.

1.5–2.4m
1.5–1.8m

ROSA 'WILLIAM LOBB'

OLD VELVET MOSS
ROSACEAE

A Moss rose with a robust deciduous nature. During midsummer it reveals large trusses of fragrant semi-double dark crimson flowers that soon fade to violet-grey. The flower buds and stalks are covered in attractive moss-like growths. It requires well-drained but moisture-retentive soil.

1.5–1.8m
1.5–1.8m

↕ height and spread   ✳ feature of interest   ▭▭▭▭ season of interest   *SHRUB AND SPECIES ROSES* **R**

CLIMBING AND RAMBLING ROSES

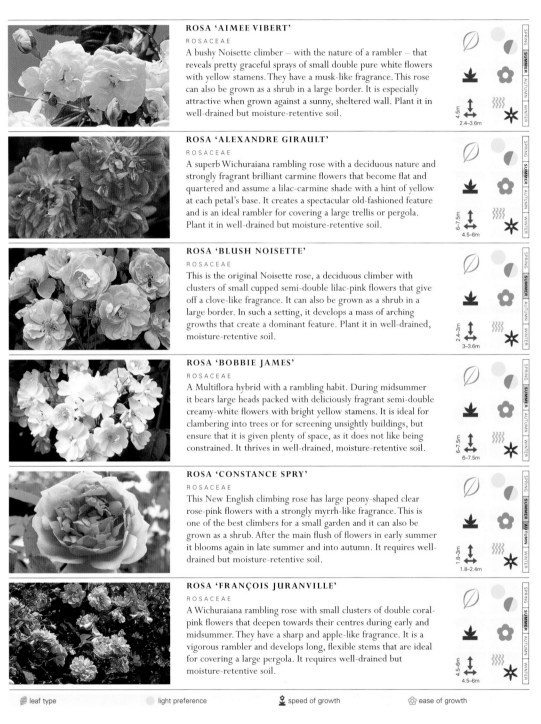

ROSA 'AIMEE VIBERT'

ROSACEAE

A bushy Noisette climber – with the nature of a rambler – that reveals pretty graceful sprays of small double pure white flowers with yellow stamens. They have a musk-like fragrance. This rose can also be grown as a shrub in a large border. It is especially attractive when grown against a sunny, sheltered wall. Plant it in well-drained but moisture-retentive soil.

4.5m
2.4–3.6m

ROSA 'ALEXANDRE GIRAULT'

ROSACEAE

A superb Wichuraiana rambling rose with a deciduous nature and strongly fragrant brilliant carmine flowers that become flat and quartered and assume a lilac-carmine shade with a hint of yellow at each petal's base. It creates a spectacular old-fashioned feature and is an ideal rambler for covering a large trellis or pergola. Plant it in well-drained but moisture-retentive soil.

6–7.5m
4.5–6m

ROSA 'BLUSH NOISETTE'

ROSACEAE

This is the original Noisette rose, a deciduous climber with clusters of small cupped semi-double lilac-pink flowers that give off a clove-like fragrance. It can also be grown as a shrub in a large border. In such a setting, it develops a mass of arching growths that create a dominant feature. Plant it in well-drained, moisture-retentive soil.

2.4–3m
3–3.6m

ROSA 'BOBBIE JAMES'

ROSACEAE

A Multiflora hybrid with a rambling habit. During midsummer it bears large heads packed with deliciously fragrant semi-double creamy-white flowers with bright yellow stamens. It is ideal for clambering into trees or for screening unsightly buildings, but ensure that it is given plenty of space, as it does not like being constrained. It thrives in well-drained, moisture-retentive soil.

6–7.5m
6–7.5m

ROSA 'CONSTANCE SPRY'

ROSACEAE

This New English climbing rose has large peony-shaped clear rose-pink flowers with a strongly myrrh-like fragrance. This is one of the best climbers for a small garden and it can also be grown as a shrub. After the main flush of flowers in early summer it blooms again in late summer and into autumn. It requires well-drained but moisture-retentive soil.

1.8–3m
1.8–2.4m

ROSA 'FRANÇOIS JURANVILLE'

ROSACEAE

A Wichuraiana rambling rose with small clusters of double coral-pink flowers that deepen towards their centres during early and midsummer. They have a sharp and apple-like fragrance. It is a vigorous rambler and develops long, flexible stems that are ideal for covering a large pergola. It requires well-drained but moisture-retentive soil.

4.5–6m
4.5–6m

leaf type   light preference   speed of growth   ease of growth

ROSA 'GERBE ROSE'
ROSACEAE

A Wichuraiana rambling rose with large clusters of double, quartered, soft pink flowers tinted with cream and borne on stiff stems. They appear mainly during midsummer and have a delicious peony-like fragrance that is especially noticeable in the evening, so plant it close to your house. It is ideal as a pillar rose and thrives in well-drained but moisture-retentive soil.

3–3.6m
2.4–3.6m

ROSA 'HELEN KNIGHT'
ROSACEAE

Also known as *Rosa ecae* 'Helen Knight', this hardy climber bears 3.5cm (1⅜in) wide bright clear yellow flowers during early summer. Its small yellowish-green leaves create an ideal foil for the flowers. It forms an ideal companion to *Clematis chrysocoma*. It flowers best when planted against a warm, sheltered wall and likes well-drained but moisture-retentive soil.

2.1–2.4m
1.5–1.8m

ROSA 'KIFTSGATE'
ROSACEAE

Also known as *Rosa filipes* 'Kiftsgate', this vigorous climber has a deciduous nature and massive heads of small single creamy-white sweetly scented flowers during early and midsummer. These are followed by small oval fruits. It is ideal for scaling trees, where it will create a feature, as well as a background for other plants. Plant it in well-drained but moisture-retentive soil.

9m
9m

ROSA 'MADAME GREGOIRE STAECHELIN'
ROSACEAE

A climbing rose with a deciduous nature and long shapely buds that open to reveal semi-double coral-pink flowers overlaid and splashed with crimson. These flowers have a delicate sweet pea fragrance and hang in large clusters from the branches. The growth is rather stiff, strong and arching, and creates a dramatic feature. Plant it in well-drained but moisture-retentive soil.

4.5–6m
3.6–4.5m

ROSA 'VEILCHENBLAU'
ROSACEAE

A Multiflora rambling rose with a deciduous nature and large trusses of small dark magenta semi-double flowers that fade to lilac. On occasion, the flowers can appear almost blue. They have a distinctive orange fragrance and are occasionally streaked with white. It is an ideal plant for training as a pillar rose. Plant it in well-drained but moisture-retentive soil.

3.6–4.5m
3.6m

ROSA 'ZEPHIRINE DROUHIN'
ROSACEAE

A climbing Bourbon rose with a deciduous nature and masses of deep rose-pink flowers throughout much of the summer. Indeed, the autumn display is often better than that of the summer. The flowers have a sweet slightly raspberry-like bouquet. It is especially suitable for growing against a cold, shady wall and needs well-drained, moisture-retentive soil.

1.8–2.7m
1.5–2.4m

⬍ height and spread   ✳ feature of interest   ▭▭▭ season of interest   *CLIMBING / RAMBLING ROSES* **R**

CLIMBERS

CLEMATIS ARMANDII
RANUNCULACEAE

A vigorous evergreen climber with a profusion of white saucer-shaped sweetly scented 5–6.5cm (2–2½in) wide flowers that appear in spring. There are several varieties, including 'Snowdrift', with large pure white flowers. Plant this clematis where the roots will be in shade. It thrives in fertile, moisture-retentive but well-drained soil.

3.6–6m / 7.5m

CLEMATIS CHRYSOCOMA
RANUNCULACEAE

A hardy deciduous climber, similar to *Clematis montana* but not so vigorous. During early and midsummer, and sometimes later, it bears single saucer-shaped white flowers, about 5cm (2in) wide, with a tinge of pink. Plant it where the roots are shaded from strong sunlight. It likes fertile, slightly alkaline, well-drained but moisture-retentive soil.

3–3.6m / 3–4.5m

CLEMATIS FLAMMULA
FRAGRANT VIRGIN'S BOWER
RANUNCULACEAE

This hardy scrambling deciduous climber creates a mass of white fragrant flowers in large, lax clusters during late summer and autumn. It develops attractive seed heads. Plant it where the roots are shaded. It thrives in fertile, slightly alkaline, moisture-retentive but well-drained soil.

3m / 1.8–2.4m

HEDERA CANARIENSIS 'GLOIRE DE MARENGO'
VARIEGATED CANARY ISLAND IVY
ARALIACEAE

Also known as *Hedera canariensis* 'Variegata', this spectacular evergreen climber develops large leathery thick leaves, deep green at their centres and merging into silvery-grey with creamy-white edges. It is ideal for creating a screen of foliage and thrives in fertile, well-drained but moisture-retentive soil.

4.5–6m / 3–4.5m

HEDERA COLCHICA 'SULPHUR HEART'
VARIEGATED PERSIAN IVY
ARALIACEAE

Also known as *Hedera colchica* 'Paddy's Pride', this vigorous, evergreen climber has large leathery broadly oval deep green leaves irregularly streaked bright yellow. It can also be grown to smother the soil in attractive leaves. It thrives in fertile, well-drained but moisture-retentive soil.

5.4–6m / 3.6–5.4m

HUMULUS LUPULUS 'AUREUS'
GOLDEN HOP
CANNABIDACEAE

A fast-growing hardy herbaceous perennial with a scrambling nature and three- to five-lobed coarsely tooth-edged bright yellowish-green leaves. In autumn the entire plant dies down to soil level and sends up fresh shoots during the following spring. It thrives in fertile, moisture-retentive soil.

1.8–3m / 1.5–2.4m

🍃 leaf type   ⬤ light preference   ♗ speed of growth   ✿ ease of growth

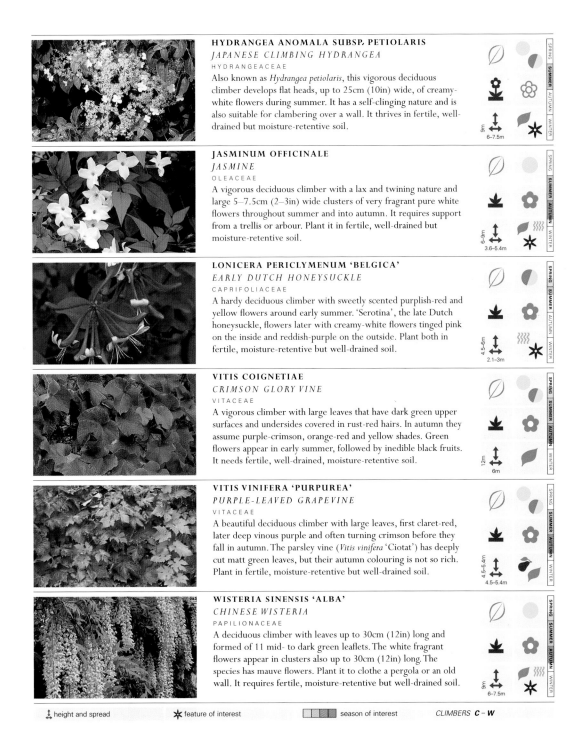

HYDRANGEA ANOMALA SUBSP. PETIOLARIS
JAPANESE CLIMBING HYDRANGEA
HYDRANGEACEAE

Also known as *Hydrangea petiolaris*, this vigorous deciduous climber develops flat heads, up to 25cm (10in) wide, of creamy-white flowers during summer. It has a self-clinging nature and is also suitable for clambering over a wall. It thrives in fertile, well-drained but moisture-retentive soil.

9m
6–7.5m

SPRING SUMMER AUTUMN WINTER

JASMINUM OFFICINALE
JASMINE
OLEACEAE

A vigorous deciduous climber with a lax and twining nature and large 5–7.5cm (2–3in) wide clusters of very fragrant pure white flowers throughout summer and into autumn. It requires support from a trellis or arbour. Plant it in fertile, well-drained but moisture-retentive soil.

6–9m
3.6–5.4m

SPRING SUMMER AUTUMN WINTER

LONICERA PERICLYMENUM 'BELGICA'
EARLY DUTCH HONEYSUCKLE
CAPRIFOLIACEAE

A hardy deciduous climber with sweetly scented purplish-red and yellow flowers around early summer. 'Serotina', the late Dutch honeysuckle, flowers later with creamy-white flowers tinged pink on the inside and reddish-purple on the outside. Plant both in fertile, moisture-retentive but well-drained soil.

4.5–6m
2.1–3m

SPRING SUMMER AUTUMN WINTER

VITIS COIGNETIAE
CRIMSON GLORY VINE
VITACEAE

A vigorous climber with large leaves that have dark green upper surfaces and undersides covered in rust-red hairs. In autumn they assume purple-crimson, orange-red and yellow shades. Green flowers appear in early summer, followed by inedible black fruits. It needs fertile, well-drained, moisture-retentive soil.

12m
6m

SPRING SUMMER AUTUMN WINTER

VITIS VINIFERA 'PURPUREA'
PURPLE-LEAVED GRAPEVINE
VITACEAE

A beautiful deciduous climber with large leaves, first claret-red, later deep vinous purple and often turning crimson before they fall in autumn. The parsley vine (*Vitis vinifera* 'Ciotat') has deeply cut matt green leaves, but their autumn colouring is not so rich. Plant in fertile, moisture-retentive but well-drained soil.

4.5–5.4m
4.5–5.4m

SPRING SUMMER AUTUMN WINTER

WISTERIA SINENSIS 'ALBA'
CHINESE WISTERIA
PAPILIONACEAE

A deciduous climber with leaves up to 30cm (12in) long and formed of 11 mid- to dark green leaflets. The white fragrant flowers appear in clusters also up to 30cm (12in) long. The species has mauve flowers. Plant it to clothe a pergola or an old wall. It requires fertile, moisture-retentive but well-drained soil.

9m
6–7.5m

SPRING SUMMER AUTUMN WINTER

⬍ height and spread   ✳ feature of interest   ▭▭▭▭ season of interest   *CLIMBERS* **C – W**

HERBS

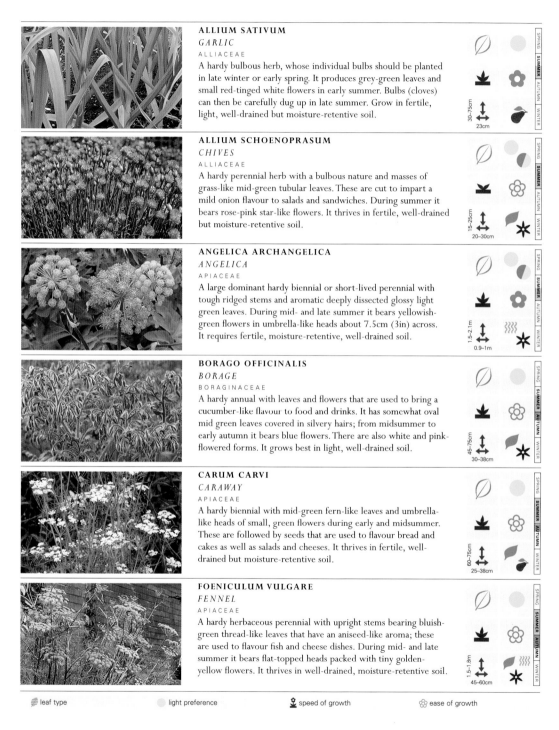

ALLIUM SATIVUM
GARLIC
ALLIACEAE

A hardy bulbous herb, whose individual bulbs should be planted in late winter or early spring. It produces grey-green leaves and small red-tinged white flowers in early summer. Bulbs (cloves) can then be carefully dug up in late summer. Grow in fertile, light, well-drained but moisture-retentive soil.

30–75cm
23cm

SPRING SUMMER AUTUMN WINTER

ALLIUM SCHOENOPRASUM
CHIVES
ALLIACEAE

A hardy perennial herb with a bulbous nature and masses of grass-like mid-green tubular leaves. These are cut to impart a mild onion flavour to salads and sandwiches. During summer it bears rose-pink star-like flowers. It thrives in fertile, well-drained but moisture-retentive soil.

15–25cm
20–30cm

SPRING SUMMER AUTUMN WINTER

ANGELICA ARCHANGELICA
ANGELICA
APIACEAE

A large dominant hardy biennial or short-lived perennial with tough ridged stems and aromatic deeply dissected glossy light green leaves. During mid- and late summer it bears yellowish-green flowers in umbrella-like heads about 7.5cm (3in) across. It requires fertile, moisture-retentive, well-drained soil.

1.5–2.1m
0.9–1m

SPRING SUMMER AUTUMN WINTER

BORAGO OFFICINALIS
BORAGE
BORAGINACEAE

A hardy annual with leaves and flowers that are used to bring a cucumber-like flavour to food and drinks. It has somewhat oval mid green leaves covered in silvery hairs; from midsummer to early autumn it bears blue flowers. There are also white and pink-flowered forms. It grows best in light, well-drained soil.

45–75cm
30–38cm

SPRING SUMMER AUTUMN WINTER

CARUM CARVI
CARAWAY
APIACEAE

A hardy biennial with mid-green fern-like leaves and umbrella-like heads of small, green flowers during early and midsummer. These are followed by seeds that are used to flavour bread and cakes as well as salads and cheeses. It thrives in fertile, well-drained but moisture-retentive soil.

60–75cm
25–38cm

SPRING SUMMER AUTUMN WINTER

FOENICULUM VULGARE
FENNEL
APIACEAE

A hardy herbaceous perennial with upright stems bearing bluish-green thread-like leaves that have an aniseed-like aroma; these are used to flavour fish and cheese dishes. During mid- and late summer it bears flat-topped heads packed with tiny golden-yellow flowers. It thrives in well-drained, moisture-retentive soil.

1.5–1.8m
45–60cm

SPRING SUMMER AUTUMN WINTER

leaf type   light preference   speed of growth   ease of growth

LAURUS NOBILIS
BAY
LAURACEAE
A hardy evergreen shrub with stiff aromatic glossy mid- to dark green leaves that are used to flavour food. Male and female flowers appear on separate plants; both are inconspicuous and yellowish-green, but purple-black berries appear only on female plants. It grows in well-drained but moisture-retentive soil.

1.8–3.6m
1.8–3.6m

MELISSA OFFICINALIS
BALM
LAMIACEAE
A hardy perennial with branching hairy stems bearing toothed and wrinkled nettle-like pale-green leaves that when bruised reveal a lemon fragrance. During early and midsummer it bears tiny white flowers. 'Aurea' (golden balm) has golden-green leaves. It needs well-drained, moisture-retentive soil.

0.6–1.2m
30–45cm

MENTHA SPICATA
SPEARMINT
LAMIACEAE
A hardy spreading herbaceous perennial with mid-green oval to lance-shaped leaves with a spearmint redolence; these are used to flavour food and drinks. It is an invasive herb and forms large clumps. Pale purple flowers appear from midsummer to early autumn. It prefers light, well-drained but moisture-retentive soil.

45–60cm
30–45cm

OCIMUM BASILICUM
BASIL
LAMIACEAE
A half-hardy annual with four-sided stems and aromatic bright green leaves with grey-green undersides. They have a strong clove-like flavour and are added to salads, soups, fish dishes and minced meat. During late summer it bears small, white flowers, and it thrives in light, well-drained but moisture-retentive soil.

45–60cm
25–38cm

SALVIA OFFICINALIS
SAGE
LAMIACEAE
A hardy evergreen shrub with oval grey-green wrinkled aromatic leaves that are used to flavour stuffings, as well as to add flavour to meat and poultry. Tubular, violet-blue flowers create a dominant display during early and midsummer. The plant requires well-drained but moisture-retentive soil.

45–60cm
45–60cm

THYMUS VULGARIS
COMMON THYME
LAMIACEAE
A hardy evergreen shrub with aromatic narrow long dark green leaves with a spicy sweet flavour. These are used dry or fresh and are added to meat and fish dishes, as well as soups and casseroles. During early summer it bears small mauve flowers. It grows well in light, well-drained but moisture-retentive soil.

10–20cm
25–30cm

SPRING SUMMER AUTUMN WINTER

⸸ height and spread   ✳ feature of interest   season of interest   *HERBS A – T*

VEGETABLES

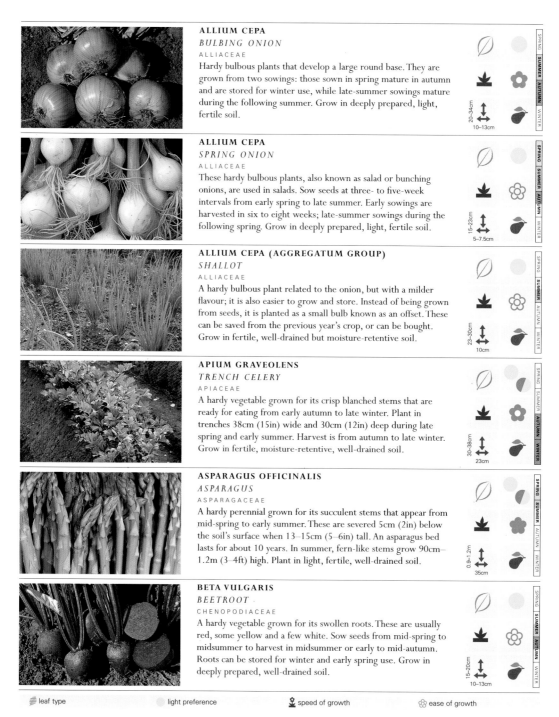

ALLIUM CEPA
BULBING ONION
ALLIACEAE
Hardy bulbous plants that develop a large round base. They are grown from two sowings: those sown in spring mature in autumn and are stored for winter use, while late-summer sowings mature during the following summer. Grow in deeply prepared, light, fertile soil.

20–34cm
10–13cm

ALLIUM CEPA
SPRING ONION
ALLIACEAE
These hardy bulbous plants, also known as salad or bunching onions, are used in salads. Sow seeds at three- to five-week intervals from early spring to late summer. Early sowings are harvested in six to eight weeks; late-summer sowings during the following spring. Grow in deeply prepared, light, fertile soil.

15–23cm
5–7.5cm

ALLIUM CEPA (AGGREGATUM GROUP)
SHALLOT
ALLIACEAE
A hardy bulbous plant related to the onion, but with a milder flavour; it is also easier to grow and store. Instead of being grown from seeds, it is planted as a small bulb known as an offset. These can be saved from the previous year's crop, or can be bought. Grow in fertile, well-drained but moisture-retentive soil.

23–30cm
10cm

APIUM GRAVEOLENS
TRENCH CELERY
APIACEAE
A hardy vegetable grown for its crisp blanched stems that are ready for eating from early autumn to late winter. Plant in trenches 38cm (15in) wide and 30cm (12in) deep during late spring and early summer. Harvest is from autumn to late winter. Grow in fertile, moisture-retentive, well-drained soil.

30–38cm
23cm

ASPARAGUS OFFICINALIS
ASPARAGUS
ASPARAGACEAE
A hardy perennial grown for its succulent stems that appear from mid-spring to early summer. These are severed 5cm (2in) below the soil's surface when 13–15cm (5–6in) tall. An asparagus bed lasts for about 10 years. In summer, fern-like stems grow 90cm–1.2m (3–4ft) high. Plant in light, fertile, well-drained soil.

0.9–1.2m
35cm

BETA VULGARIS
BEETROOT
CHENOPODIACEAE
A hardy vegetable grown for its swollen roots. These are usually red, some yellow and a few white. Sow seeds from mid-spring to midsummer to harvest in midsummer or early to mid-autumn. Roots can be stored for winter and early spring use. Grow in deeply prepared, well-drained soil.

15–20cm
10–13cm

≣ leaf type   ● light preference   ⚘ speed of growth   ❀ ease of growth

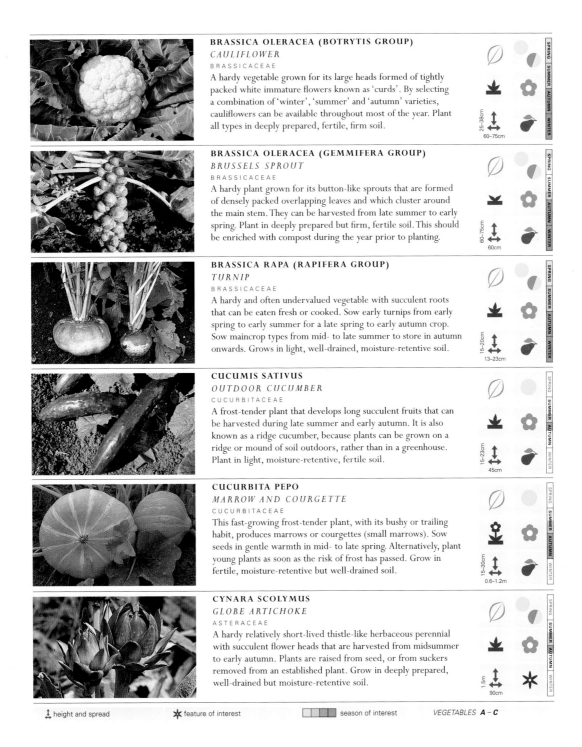

BRASSICA OLERACEA (BOTRYTIS GROUP)
CAULIFLOWER
BRASSICACEAE

A hardy vegetable grown for its large heads formed of tightly packed white immature flowers known as 'curds'. By selecting a combination of 'winter', 'summer' and 'autumn' varieties, cauliflowers can be available throughout most of the year. Plant all types in deeply prepared, fertile, firm soil.

25–38cm
60–75cm

BRASSICA OLERACEA (GEMMIFERA GROUP)
BRUSSELS SPROUT
BRASSICACEAE

A hardy plant grown for its button-like sprouts that are formed of densely packed overlapping leaves and which cluster around the main stem. They can be harvested from late summer to early spring. Plant in deeply prepared but firm, fertile soil. This should be enriched with compost during the year prior to planting.

60–75cm
60cm

BRASSICA RAPA (RAPIFERA GROUP)
TURNIP
BRASSICACEAE

A hardy and often undervalued vegetable with succulent roots that can be eaten fresh or cooked. Sow early turnips from early spring to early summer for a late spring to early autumn crop. Sow maincrop types from mid- to late summer to store in autumn onwards. Grows in light, well-drained, moisture-retentive soil.

15–20cm
13–23cm

CUCUMIS SATIVUS
OUTDOOR CUCUMBER
CUCURBITACEAE

A frost-tender plant that develops long succulent fruits that can be harvested during late summer and early autumn. It is also known as a ridge cucumber, because plants can be grown on a ridge or mound of soil outdoors, rather than in a greenhouse. Plant in light, moisture-retentive, fertile soil.

15–23cm
45cm

CUCURBITA PEPO
MARROW AND COURGETTE
CUCURBITACEAE

This fast-growing frost-tender plant, with its bushy or trailing habit, produces marrows or courgettes (small marrows). Sow seeds in gentle warmth in mid- to late spring. Alternatively, plant young plants as soon as the risk of frost has passed. Grow in fertile, moisture-retentive but well-drained soil.

15–30cm
0.6–1.2m

CYNARA SCOLYMUS
GLOBE ARTICHOKE
ASTERACEAE

A hardy relatively short-lived thistle-like herbaceous perennial with succulent flower heads that are harvested from midsummer to early autumn. Plants are raised from seed, or from suckers removed from an established plant. Grow in deeply prepared, well-drained but moisture-retentive soil.

1.5m
90cm

⬍ height and spread   ✳ feature of interest   ▭▭▭ season of interest   *VEGETABLES* **A – C**

VEGETABLES

DAUCUS CAROTA
CARROT
APIACEAE

A hardy vegetable grown for its swollen roots that can be cooked or grated and added to salads. Short-rooted carrots are used for early crops, while intermediate (blunt-ended and medium-sized) and long-rooted (long, tapering and pointed) varieties are best for late sowing. Grow in deeply prepared, stone-free soil.

10–20cm
5–10cm

LACTUCA SATIVA
LETTUCE
ASTERACEAE

A popular salad vegetable of several forms: cabbage types include butterheads (globular and soft-leaved) and crispheads (round, crisp heads). Cos types are upright, with crisp leaves, while loose leaf types have a mass of leaves that can be harvested individually. Plant in fertile, well-drained, moisture-retentive soil.

15–23cm
23–30cm

LYCOPERSICON ESCULENTUM
OUTDOOR TOMATO
SOLANACEAE

Tomatoes are fruits but are always grouped with vegetables. There are two forms of these frost-tender plants: cordon varieties are supported with canes and their side shoots removed, bush types do not need support and they keep their side shoots. Plant both in fertile, light, moisture-retentive, well-drained soil.

0.9–1.2m
60–75cm

PASTINACA SATIVA
PARSNIP
PAPILIONACEAE

A hardy vegetable with firm swollen roots for harvesting from mid-autumn to late winter or early spring. It is a much neglected vegetable but one that is easy to grow. The flavour of the roots is improved by frost. Grow in deeply prepared, fertile and well-drained soil.

23–30cm
15–20cm

PHASEOLUS COCCINEUS
RUNNER BEAN
PAPILIONACEAE

This popular frost-tender vegetable is widely grown and, as well as being an edible plant, creates an attractive screen. The usual form climbs 2.4–3m (8–10ft) high and is also known as stick bean, while dwarf runner beans form bushes 45cm (18in) high. Grow in fertile, moisture-retentive but well-drained soil.

0.45–3m
30–38cm

PHASEOLUS VULGARIS
FRENCH BEAN
PAPILIONACEAE

A frost-tender vegetable that develops succulent beans for harvesting from midsummer to mid-autumn. Most varieties form low bushes that do not need support, but there are a few that clamber and require supports that reach about 1.8m (6ft) high. Grow in fertile, moisture-retentive but well-drained soil.

0.5–1.8m
30–38cm

SPRING SUMMER AUTUMN WINTER

leaf type   light preference   speed of growth   ease of growth

PISUM SATIVUM
GARDEN PEA
PAPILIONACEAE

A traditional vegetable bearing pods that enclose tender and sweet peas; pods are harvested from late spring to mid-autumn, depending on the variety. Sow seeds 7.5cm apart in three staggered rows, in trenches 5cm (2in) deep and 23cm (9in) wide. Grow in deeply prepared, moisture-retentive, well-drained soil.

30–90cm
25–30cm

RAPHANUS SATIVUS
RADISH
CRUCIFERAE

Radishes are grown for their swollen cylindrical or globular roots. Summer types are eaten raw in salads; winter varieties are cooked or pickled. Sow summer types every few weeks from early to late spring or early summer, and winter ones during midsummer for lifting in mid-autumn, then storing.

10–15cm
5–15cm

SOLANUM MELONGENA
AUBERGINE
SOLANACEAE

A subtropical frost-tender plant, usually grown in a greenhouse but also outdoors in warm sunny sheltered areas. Large cloches help to give protection against cold winds. There are several varieties, with skin colours including black, white and purple. Grow in large pots or growing-bags on a warm, sheltered patio.

30–45cm
30–45cm

SPINACIA OLERACEA
SPINACH
CHENOPODIACEAE

This plant is grown for its leaves. There are two main types – summer and winter. Sow seeds of summer spinach from early spring to early summer; harvesting eight to ten weeks later. Sow winter spinach in late summer or early autumn; harvesting 12 to 15 weeks later. Grow both in fertile, well-drained soil.

20–30cm
25–30cm

VICIA FABA
BROAD BEAN
PAPILIONACEAE

A vegetable with square stems that bear large pods of succulent beans, which are harvested from the latter part of early summer to early autumn. Sowing is done during spring. Most varieties are 1.2m (4ft) high, while dwarf ones are 30–45cm (12–18in). Grow in light, fertile, well-drained but moisture-retentive soil.

0.3–1.2m
30–50cm

ZEA MAYS
SWEETCORN
GRAMINEAE

Often known as maize or corn, this frost-tender plant produces heads packed with bright yellow seeds. These are ready for harvesting during late summer and early autumn. Cook or freeze heads soon after they have been harvested. Grow in deeply prepared, fertile, moisture-retentive but well-drained soil.

1.2–1.8m
45cm

SPRING SUMMER AUTUMN WINTER

⤡ height and spread   ✳ feature of interest   ▭ season of interest   *VEGETABLES* **D–Z**

FRUIT

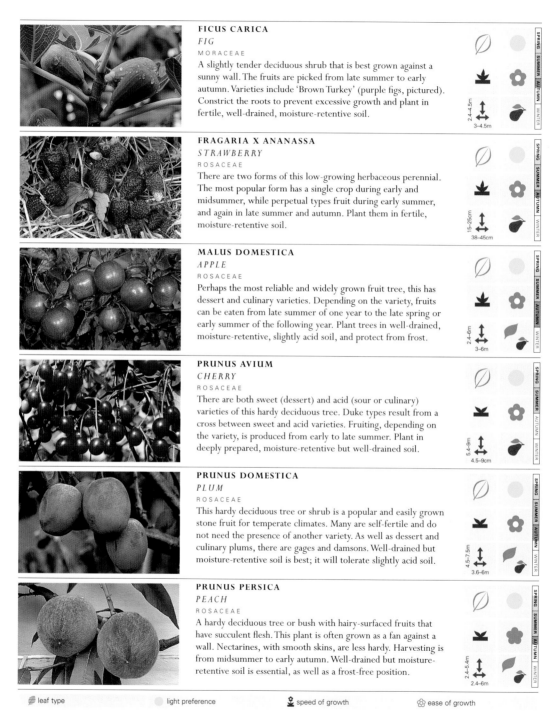

FICUS CARICA
FIG
MORACEAE

A slightly tender deciduous shrub that is best grown against a sunny wall. The fruits are picked from late summer to early autumn. Varieties include 'Brown Turkey' (purple figs, pictured). Constrict the roots to prevent excessive growth and plant in fertile, well-drained, moisture-retentive soil.

2.4–4.5m
3–4.5m

SPRING SUMMER AUTUMN WINTER

FRAGARIA X ANANASSA
STRAWBERRY
ROSACEAE

There are two forms of this low-growing herbaceous perennial. The most popular form has a single crop during early and midsummer, while perpetual types fruit during early summer, and again in late summer and autumn. Plant them in fertile, moisture-retentive soil.

15–25cm
38–45cm

SPRING SUMMER AUTUMN WINTER

MALUS DOMESTICA
APPLE
ROSACEAE

Perhaps the most reliable and widely grown fruit tree, this has dessert and culinary varieties. Depending on the variety, fruits can be eaten from late summer of one year to the late spring or early summer of the following year. Plant trees in well-drained, moisture-retentive, slightly acid soil, and protect from frost.

2.4–6m
3–6m

SPRING SUMMER AUTUMN WINTER

PRUNUS AVIUM
CHERRY
ROSACEAE

There are both sweet (dessert) and acid (sour or culinary) varieties of this hardy deciduous tree. Duke types result from a cross between sweet and acid varieties. Fruiting, depending on the variety, is produced from early to late summer. Plant in deeply prepared, moisture-retentive but well-drained soil.

5.4–9m
4.5–9cm

SPRING SUMMER AUTUMN WINTER

PRUNUS DOMESTICA
PLUM
ROSACEAE

This hardy deciduous tree or shrub is a popular and easily grown stone fruit for temperate climates. Many are self-fertile and do not need the presence of another variety. As well as dessert and culinary plums, there are gages and damsons. Well-drained but moisture-retentive soil is best; it will tolerate slightly acid soil.

4.5–7.5m
3.6–6m

SPRING SUMMER AUTUMN WINTER

PRUNUS PERSICA
PEACH
ROSACEAE

A hardy deciduous tree or bush with hairy-surfaced fruits that have succulent flesh. This plant is often grown as a fan against a wall. Nectarines, with smooth skins, are less hardy. Harvesting is from midsummer to early autumn. Well-drained but moisture-retentive soil is essential, as well as a frost-free position.

2.4–4.5m
2.4–6m

SPRING SUMMER AUTUMN WINTER

🍃 leaf type   ⬤ light preference   ⚓ speed of growth   ✿ ease of growth

PYRUS COMMUNIS
PEAR
ROSACEAE

A hardy deciduous tree or shrub that has culinary and dessert varieties that can be eaten from late summer to midwinter. It can be grown as a tree, bush or against a wall. Well-drained but moisture-retentive soil is essential. Also, try to shelter the plant from cold wind, especially in spring.

3–6m
3.6–6m

SPRING SUMMER AUTUMN WINTER

RIBES NIGRUM
BLACKCURRANT
GROSSULARIACEAE

An easily grown hardy deciduous shrub that produces succulent black fruits ready for picking from midsummer to early autumn, depending on the variety. A fertile, moisture-retentive soil is absolutely essential to encourage the yearly production of the fruit-bearing shoots.

1.2–1.5m
1.2–1.5m

SPRING SUMMER AUTUMN WINTER

RIBES RUBRUM
REDCURRANT
GROSSULARIACEAE

A hardy deciduous bush that has a less vigorous nature than a blackcurrant. The bush has a short stem (leg) and develops fruit on a permanent framework of branches from mid- to late summer. Plant in moderately fertile, well-drained but moisture-retentive soil. It benefits from a wind-sheltered position.

1.5m
1.2–1.5m

SPRING SUMMER AUTUMN WINTER

RIBES UVA-CRISPA
GOOSEBERRY
GROSSULARIACEAE

A popular hardy deciduous bush that has succulent berries from early to late summer, depending on the variety. Bushes are grown on a short stem (leg), which supports a permanent framework of branches. The plant can also be grown as a cordon. Place it in well-drained but moisture-retentive soil in a sheltered position.

0.9–1.5m
0.9–1.5m

SPRING SUMMER AUTUMN WINTER

RUBUS FRUTICOSUS
BLACKBERRY
ROSACEAE

A popular hardy deciduous cane fruit with a wide range of varieties that produce berries from midsummer to early autumn. Hybrid berries, such as tayberries, loganberries and boysenberries, are also popular. Fertile, well-drained but moisture-retentive soil is essential to encourage yearly shoots.

1.8–2.1m
3–3.6m

SPRING SUMMER AUTUMN WINTER

RUBUS IDAEUS
RASPBERRY
ROSACEAE

This hardy deciduous cane fruit is well known. There are two types: the most popular is summer-fruiting, with fruits from mid- to late summer, depending on the variety. Autumn-fruiting types bear berries during late summer and into autumn. Plant both types in fertile, moisture-retentive but well-drained soil.

1.8m
1.8m

SPRING SUMMER AUTUMN WINTER

⬍ height and spread   ✳ feature of interest   ▭▭▭ season of interest   *FRUIT* **F – R**

HEDGING PLANTS

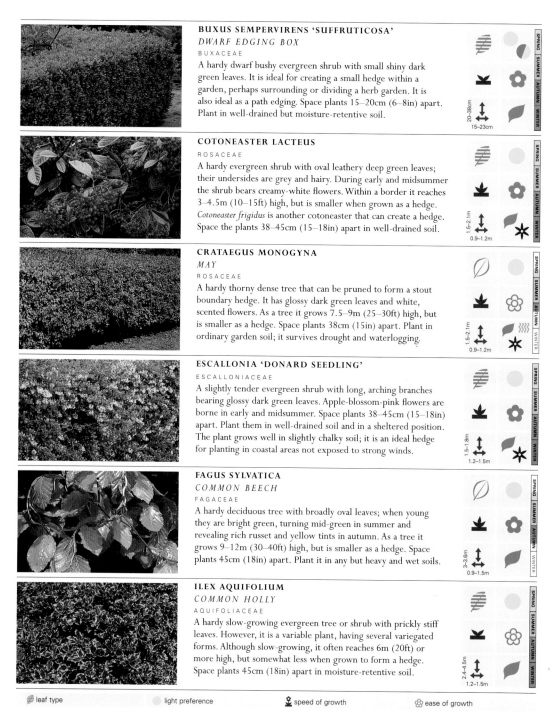

BUXUS SEMPERVIRENS 'SUFFRUTICOSA'
DWARF EDGING BOX
BUXACEAE
A hardy dwarf bushy evergreen shrub with small shiny dark green leaves. It is ideal for creating a small hedge within a garden, perhaps surrounding or dividing a herb garden. It is also ideal as a path edging. Space plants 15–20cm (6–8in) apart. Plant in well-drained but moisture-retentive soil.

20–38cm
15–23cm

COTONEASTER LACTEUS
ROSACEAE
A hardy evergreen shrub with oval leathery deep green leaves; their undersides are grey and hairy. During early and midsummer the shrub bears creamy-white flowers. Within a border it reaches 3–4.5m (10–15ft) high, but is smaller when grown as a hedge. *Cotoneaster frigidus* is another cotoneaster that can create a hedge. Space the plants 38–45cm (15–18in) apart in well-drained soil.

1.5–2.1m
0.9–1.2m

CRATAEGUS MONOGYNA
MAY
ROSACEAE
A hardy thorny dense tree that can be pruned to form a stout boundary hedge. It has glossy dark green leaves and white, scented flowers. As a tree it grows 7.5–9m (25–30ft) high, but is smaller as a hedge. Space plants 38cm (15in) apart. Plant in ordinary garden soil; it survives drought and waterlogging.

1.5–2.1m
0.9–1.2m

ESCALLONIA 'DONARD SEEDLING'
ESCALLONIACEAE
A slightly tender evergreen shrub with long, arching branches bearing glossy dark green leaves. Apple-blossom-pink flowers are borne in early and midsummer. Space plants 38–45cm (15–18in) apart. Plant them in well-drained soil and in a sheltered position. The plant grows well in slightly chalky soil; it is an ideal hedge for planting in coastal areas not exposed to strong winds.

1.5–1.8m
1.2–1.5m

FAGUS SYLVATICA
COMMON BEECH
FAGACEAE
A hardy deciduous tree with broadly oval leaves; when young they are bright green, turning mid-green in summer and revealing rich russet and yellow tints in autumn. As a tree it grows 9–12m (30–40ft) high, but is smaller as a hedge. Space plants 45cm (18in) apart. Plant it in any but heavy and wet soils.

3–3.6m
0.9–1.5m

ILEX AQUIFOLIUM
COMMON HOLLY
AQUIFOLIACEAE
A hardy slow-growing evergreen tree or shrub with prickly stiff leaves. However, it is a variable plant, having several variegated forms. Although slow-growing, it often reaches 6m (20ft) or more high, but somewhat less when grown to form a hedge. Space plants 45cm (18in) apart in moisture-retentive soil.

2.4–4.5m
1.2–1.5m

leaf type   light preference   speed of growth   ease of growth

LAVANDULA ANGUSTIFOLIA 'HIDCOTE'
LAVENDER
LAMIACEAE

A moderately hardy dwarf evergreen shrub with aromatic narrow silvery-green leaves and pale grey-blue flowers borne in clusters from midsummer to early autumn. It forms a short-lived hedge; after about five years, plants become bare at their bases. Space plants 23–30cm (9–12in) apart in well-drained soil.

30–60cm
45–60cm

LONICERA NITIDA 'BAGGESON'S GOLD'
GOLDEN CHINESE HONEYSUCKLE
CAPRIFOLIACEAE

A hardy bushy evergreen shrub with small golden leaves that become yellowish-green in autumn. It has a relaxed nature and instead of clipping it with hedging shears it is best to prune it occasionally with secateurs. Space plants 25–30cm (10–12in) apart in well-drained but moisture-retentive soil.

1–1.5m
75–90cm

ROSA 'THE QUEEN ELIZABETH'
ROSE
ROSACEAE

Also known as 'Queen Elizabeth', this disease-resistant Floribunda rose has a vigorous upright nature. During early and midsummer — and often again later — it bears slightly fragrant clear-pink flowers amid dark green, glossy leaves. Plant 45cm (18in) apart in well-drained but moisture-retentive soil.

1.8m
1.2m

ROSMARINUS OFFICINALIS
ROSEMARY
LAMIACEAE

A hardy evergreen shrub with aromatic narrow dark green leaves with white undersides. During spring it bears mauve flowers, which continue to appear sporadically until early autumn. Space plants 38cm (15in) apart to form an informal hedge. Plant in a well-drained soil.

1.5–2.1m
1.2–1.5m

TAXUS BACCATA
YEW
TAXACEAE

A hardy slow-growing evergreen conifer with stiff narrow dark green leaves that are yellow-green underneath. As a tree it grows about 4.5m (15ft) high, but is smaller as a hedge. Space plants 38–45cm (15–18in) apart. It thrives in most soils, except those that are exceptionally wet.

1.8–2.4m
75–90cm

THUJA PLICATA
WESTERN RED CEDAR
CUPRESSACEAE

A hardy evergreen fast-growing and long-lived conifer with bright glossy green leaves. When grown as a tree it eventually reaches more than 12m (40ft) high, but much less as a hedge. It forms a superb perimeter screen. Space plants 45–60cm (18–24in) apart in well-drained but moisture-retentive soil.

2.1–2.4m
1–1.2m

SPRING | SUMMER | AUTUMN | WINTER

↕ height and spread   ✳ feature of interest   ▮▮▮ season of interest   *HEDGING PLANTS* **B – T**

GLOSSARY

ALPINE: A plant that in its natural mountain habitat grows above the uppermost limit of trees. More colloquially, plants that are suitable for rock gardens are called alpines.

ANNUAL: A plant that grows from seed, flowers and dies within the same year. Some half-hardy perennial plants are grown as annuals in frost-prone climates.

AQUATIC PLANT: A plant that lives totally or partly submerged in water.

AXIL: The upper angle between leaf and stem.

BEDDING PLANTS: Plants that are set out for a temporary seasonal displays and discarded at the end of the season.

BIENNIAL: A plant raised from seed that makes its initial growth in one year and produces flowers during the following one, then dies.

BOG-GARDEN PLANTS: Plants that live with their roots in moist soil.

BULB: An underground food storage organ formed of fleshy, modified leaves that enclose a dormant shoot.

CALYX: The outer and protective part of a flower. It is usually green and is very apparent in roses.

COMPOST: Vegetable waste from kitchens, as well as soft parts of garden plants, which is encouraged to decompose and to form a material that can be dug into soil or used to create a mulch around plants.

CORM: An underground storage organ formed of a swollen stem base, as in, for example, a crocus.

CULTIVAR: A shortened term for 'cultivated variety' that indicates a variety raised in cultivation. Strictly speaking, most modern varieties are cultivars, but the term 'variety' is still widely used because it is familiar to most gardeners.

CUTTING: A section of plant which is detached and encouraged to form roots and stems to provide a new independent plant. Cuttings may be taken from roots, stems or leaves.

DEAD-HEADING: The removal of a faded flower head to prevent the formation of seeds and to encourage the development of further flowers.

DORMANT: When a plant is alive but is making no growth, it is called dormant. The dormant period is usually the winter.

EVERGREEN: Plants that appear to be green throughout the year and not to lose their leaves are called evergreen. In reality, however, they shed some of their leaves throughout the year, while producing others.

FRIABLE: Soil that is crumbly and light and easily worked. The term especially applies to soil being prepared as a seedbed in spring.

HALF-HARDY: A plant that can withstand fairly low temperatures, but needs protection from frost.

HALF-HARDY ANNUAL: An annual that is sown in gentle warmth in a greenhouse in spring, the seedlings being transferred to wider spacings in pots or boxes. The plants are placed in a garden or container only when all risk of frost has passed.

HARDEN OFF: Gradually accustoming plants to cooler conditions so that they can be planted outside.

HARDY: A plant that is able to survive outdoors in winter. In the case of some rock-garden plants, good drainage is essential to ensure their survival.

HERB: A plant that is grown for its aromatic qualities and can often be used in cooking or medicine.

HERBACEOUS PERENNIAL: A plant with no woody tissue that lives for several years, usually dying down in winter. It may be deciduous or evergreen.

HYBRID: A cross between two different species, varieties or genera of plants.

LOAM: Friable mixture of sand, silt and clay.

MARGINAL PLANTS: Plants that live in shallow water at the edges of ponds or in boggy soil around them.

MULCHING: Covering the soil around plants with well decayed organic material such as garden compost, peat or, in the case of rock garden plants, stone chippings or 6mm (¼in) shingle.

NEUTRAL: Soil that is neither acid nor alkaline, with a pH of 7.0, is said to be neutral. Most plants grow in a pH of about 6.5.

PEAT: A naturally occurring substance formed from partly rotted organic material in water-logged soils, used as a growing medium and soil additive.

PERENNIAL: Any plant that lives for three or more years is called a perennial.

PERGOLA: An open timber structure made up of linked arches.

POTTING COMPOST: Traditionally, a compost formed of loam, sharp sand and peat, fertilizers and chalk. The ratio of the ingredients is altered according to whether the compost is used for sowing seeds, potting-up or repotting plants into larger containers. Recognition of the environmental importance of conserving peat beds has led to many modern composts being formed of other organic materials, such as coir or shredded bark.

PRICKING OUT: Transplanting seedlings from the container in which they were sown to one where they are more widely spaced.

RACEME: An elongated flower head with each flower having a stem.

RAISED BED: A raised area, that is encircled by a wall or other barrier. Rock garden plants can be grown both in the raised bed and the wall.

RHIZOME: An underground or partly buried horizontal stem that can be slender or fleshy. Some irises have thick fleshy rhizomes, while those of lily-of-the-valley are slender and creeping. They act as storage organs and perpetuate plants from one season to another.

SCREE BED: An area formed of layers of rubble, gravel and compost, imitating naturally occurring areas of scree.

SEED LEAVES: The first leaves that develop on a seedling, which are coarser and more robust than the true leaves.

SEMI-EVERGREEN: A plant that may keep all or some of its leaves in a reasonably mild winter.

SINK GARDENS: Old stone sinks partly filled with drainage material and then with freely draining compost. They are planted with miniature conifers and bulbs, as well as small rock-garden plants. These features are usually displayed on terraces and patios.

SPECIES ROSE: A common term for a wild rose or one of its near relatives.

STAMEN: The male part of a flower.

STANDARD: A tree or shrub trained to form a rounded head of branches at the top of a clear stem.

SUB-SHRUB: Small and spreading shrub with a woody base. It differs from normal shrubs in that when grown in temperate regions its upper stems and shoots die back during winter.

TENDER: A plant which will not tolerate temperatures below freezing is referred to as tender.

TOPSOIL: The uppermost layer of soil which is structured and contains organic matter and humus.

TUBER: A swollen, thickened and fleshy stem or root. Some tubers are swollen roots (dahlia), while others are swollen stems (potato). They serve as storage organs and help to perpetuate plants from one season to another.

VARIEGATED: Usually applied to leaves and used to describe a state of having two or more colours.

VARIETY: A naturally occurring variation of a species that retains its characteristics when propagated. The term is often used for cultivars.

WILDLIFE POND: An informal pond, often positioned towards the far end of a garden, which encourages the presence of wildlife such as frogs, birds, insects and small mammals.

INDEX

ACKNOWLEDGEMENTS

t *top*   **b** *below*   **l** *left*   **r** *right*   **Directory a–f**, *starting from top*

Liz Eddison 14t, 22, 28l, 29r, 30l, 31r, 32r, 33l, r, 34r, 53;

The Garden Picture Library / David Askham 94f / Brian Carter 81a /
David England 106e / Christopher Gallagher 104f / John Glover 89b /
Sunnvia Harte 70d / Neil Holmes 85a / Jacqui Hurst 63b / Lamontagne 100b, 101e /
Howard Rice 91d, 106b / David Russell 94c / Alec Scaresbrook 100c / JS Sira 90c /
Friedrich Strauss 99d / Mel Watson 97b;

John Glover 1 & 26–27, 2 & 18, 4 & 24, 5, 6 & 112, 7, 10–11, 12t, b, 13, 16t, 16b, 20,
28r, 29l, 30r, 31l, 32l, 35l, r, 36, 38, 41, 43, 45, 47, 54, 56, 58–59 / Rupert Golby 51 /
Alan Titchmarsh 14b, 15, 17, 34l;

Peter McHoy 63c,d, 66c,e, 67b, 68f, 71b,f, 74e, 75a,b, 76d, 78d,e, 80a, 81c,d, 86b, 88b,
89f, 90a,b,f, 91f, 92f, 96f, 97c,d, 101f, 104c, 105e, 106c, 107f;

The Harry Smith Collection 62a,c,d,e,f, 63a, 64a,c,d,e, 65b,c,e,f, 66a,b,d,e, 67a,c,d,e,f,
68a,b,c,e, 69a,b,d,e,f, 70a,b,c,e,f, 71c,d,e, 72b,c,d,f, 73a,b,d,f, 74b,c,d,f, 75c,d,e,f,
76a,b,c,e,f, 77a,c,d,e,f, 78a,b,c,f, 79b,c,d,e,f, 80b,c,d,e,f, 81b,e,f, 82b,c,d,e,
83a,b,c,d,e, 84b,c,d,e,f, 85c,d,e,f, 86a,c,d,e,f, 87a,c,d,e,f, 88c,d,f, 89a,c,d,e, 91a,b,c,e,
92a,b,c,d,e, 93a,b,d,e,f, 94a,b,d,e, 95a,b,c,d,e,f, 96a,b,c,d, 97a,e,f, 98b,c,d,e,f, 99f,
100a,d,e,f, 101a,b,c,d, 102a,b,c,d,e,f, 103a,b,c,d,e,f, 104a,b,d,e, 105a,b,c,d,f, 106a,d,
107a,b,c,d,e;

David Squire 62b, 63e,f, 64b,f, 65a,d, 68d, 69c, 71a, 72a,e, 73c,e, 74a, 77b, 79a, 82a,f,
83f, 84a, 85b, 87b, 88a,e, 90d,e, 93c, 96e, 99a,b,c,e, 106f.